Young
2004 POETRY C

ONCE UPON A RHYME

IMAGINATION FOR A NEW GENERATION

CW00322722

Southern Scotland Vol II
Edited by Annabel Cook

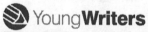 Young**Writers**

First published in Great Britain in 2004 by:
Young Writers
Remus House
Coltsfoot Drive
Peterborough
PE2 9JX
Telephone: 01733 890066
Website: www.youngwriters.co.uk

SB ISBN 1 84460 593 0

Foreword

Young Writers was established in 1991 and has been passionately devoted to the promotion of reading and writing in children and young adults ever since. The quest continues today. Young Writers remains as committed to engendering the fostering of burgeoning poetic and literary talent as ever.

This year's Young Writers competition has proven as vibrant and dynamic as ever and we are delighted to present a showcase of the best poetry from across the UK. Each poem has been carefully selected from a wealth of *Once Upon A Rhyme* entries before ultimately being published in this, our twelfth primary school poetry series.

Once again, we have been supremely impressed by the overall high quality of the entries we have received. The imagination, energy and creativity which has gone into each young writer's entry made choosing the best poems a challenging and often difficult but ultimately hugely rewarding task - the general high standard of the work submitted amply vindicating this opportunity to bring their poetry to a larger appreciative audience.

We sincerely hope you are pleased with our final selection and that you will enjoy *Once Upon A Rhyme Southern Scotland Vol II* for many years to come.

Contents

Kelsey Bannatyne (8)   16
Tracey Fisher (10)   17
Chloe Rose (9)   17
Alastair Leghorn (10)   18

Cliftonhall School, Newbridge
Alan Garden (10)   18
Jamie Maclachlan (9)   19
Thomas Short (9)   20
Alex-Jade Donaldson (9)   21
Donald Patrick (9)   22
Katie Matthews (10)   23

Closeburn Primary School, Thornhill
Ariadne Weir (10)   24
Adele Queen (11)   24
Michael McAleavey (10)   24
Callum Anderson (11)   25
Dale McGenily (11)   25
Catherine Moodycliffe (10)   25
Maimie Sloan (10)   26
David Kennedy (11)   26
Matthew McMillan (9)   26
Grace Dale (9)   27
Elisha Scott (10)   27
Ariane Porter (10)   27
Emily Count-Stewart (10)   28
Samantha Keene (11)   28
Jack Howat (9)   28
Alice Findlater (11)   29
Kirsty Clark (11)   29
Loren Rammell (12)   29
Michael Blunsden (11)   30

Craigour Park Primary School, Edinburgh
Lynsey Keegan   30
Gemma Bartie (11)   31
Paul McGinnity (11)   31
Brett Clayton (10)   32
Tara Blackley (10)   32
Paul Grant (10)   33

Crawforddyke Primary School, Carluke

Kurtis McLeod (12)	33
Marc Muir (11)	34
Vicky Cumming (12)	34
Adele Johnston & Melissa Brownlee (11)	34
Hannah Thomson (8)	35
Kerry Reid (11)	35
Eilidh Carmichael (12) & Stephanie Walker (11)	36
Hannah Robertson (8)	36
Lisa Rattray (12)	37
Scott Melvin (11)	38
Ashley Wigston (11)	38
Kirsten Stuart (11)	39
Shari Nicol (12)	39

Cumbernauld Primary School, Cumbernauld

Rebecca McGuire (11)	40
Adam Smith (11)	40
Dionne Wilson (10)	40
Ryan Dynes (10)	41
Susannah Beattie (11)	41
Jordan Stewart (11)	42
Aimeé Pollock (11)	42
Eilish Barrett (11)	42
Scott McFaulds (11)	43
Siobhan Black (10)	43
Euan Calder (10)	43
Johnathon Yau (10)	44
Gary Love (11)	44
Samantha Little (11)	45
Andrew Mooney (11)	45
Andrew MacQueen (10)	46
Emma Sommerville (10)	46
Lauren Pickering (12)	47
Tom Robertson (11)	47
Anthony Morgan (12)	48
Scott Greenlees (11)	48
Rebecca Wilson (12)	48

Drumlemble Primary School, Campbeltown

Grant Kilby (10)	49
Scott Anderson (10)	49
Christopher Lang (10)	49
Greg Newlands (10)	50
David Crawford (11)	50
Graeme McMillan (10)	50
Lindsey Armour (9)	51
Jennifer Kelly (10)	51
Ben Craig (10)	51
Andrew McClement (9)	52
Catherine Armour (11)	52
Lorna Armour (11)	53
James Cairns (9)	53
Adam Bellamy (11)	54
Eilidh Gaughan (9)	54
Louise Mitchell (10)	55
Alison Millar (10)	55
Tiffany Lang (8)	55
Kerr Gaughan (11)	56

Drummore Primary School, Stranraer

Lauren Ward (10)	56
Shaun Slavin (10)	57
Scott Hose (11)	58
Kara Torrance (12)	59
Jennifer McClintick (10)	60

Dalintober Primary School, Campbeltown

Rebecca MacPherson (9)	60
Kerry McDougall (11)	61

Gilmourton Primary School, Strathaven

Gavin Dunbar (11)	61
Jill Naismith (9)	62
Rhiah McLean (10)	62
Rachel Naismith (11)	63
Martin Cowan (10)	63
Peter Hastings (11)	64
Erin Hastings (9)	64

Victoria Lennox (9)   65
Jaimie Crozer (10)   65

Glenluce Primary School, Newton Stewart
Mitchell Saunders (8)   66
Caitlin Davis (7)   66
Jenni Hastie (9)   66
Caty Cameron (8)   67
Lorna Rae (9)   67
Emma Miskimmins (9)   67
Hannah McIntosh (9)   68
Caroline McQuistin (8)   68
Morgan McIlwrick (9)   68
Rorie White (8)   69
Eve Spears (11)   69
Shona Rennie (11)   70
Elizabeth Crawfurd (8)   70
Kirstie McHarrie (12)   71
Sophie Forster (9)   71
Ewan Cameron (11)   72
Kayley McKie (11)   72
Lauren McQuistin (11)   73
Andrew King (10)   73
Laura Paterson (11)   74
Ruth Smedley (12)   74
Chelsea Aitken (11)   75
Callum Miskimmins (11)   75
Henry Crawfurd (11)   76
Kay Wilson (11)   76

Inchinnan Primary School, Inchinnan
Hannah Mathieson & Fiona Caldwell (10)   77
Arran Dulai (11)   77
Dylan Connor & Darran Sims (10)   78
Fraser Reid (10) & Stephen McColl (11)   78
Ryan Adam (10)   78
Christopher Keown (11)   79
Stewart Fox & Courtney McClure (10)   79
Callum Blair & Stewart Brown (10)   79
Kayleigh Nardini & Gemma Westwood (10)   80
Nicola Sheerin & Danuta McPherson (10)   80

David Mimnagh (10) & Lewis Kerr (11)   80
Callum McGregor (10) & Daniel Wilson (11)   81
Greg McBride, Kyle McCrae & Johnny Morrison (10)   81

Kilchrenan Primary School, Taynuilt
Georgia Todd (9)   81
Jade Sutherland (11)   82
Euan Meldrum (9)   82
Chloe Wilkie (11)   83
Benjamin Bartholomew (8)   83
Joy Palmer (8)   84
Jodi Sutherland (8)   84
Sarah Wilkie (8)   85
Calum Galbraith (10)   85
Aron Wright (10)   86
Joshua Bartholomew (8)   86
Niall Sinclair (11)   87
Callum Leitch (10)   87

Kirkshaws Primary School, Coatbridge
Adam Blades (8)   88
Mark Cappie (8)   88
Amanda McFarlane (8)   88
Melissa Moran (9)   89
Connor Bruin (8)   89
Sean Gallacher (8)   89
Conlon Campbell (8)   90
Amy Brannen (8)   90

Musselburgh Burgh Primary School, Musselburgh
Hannah Penman (9)   90
Craig Milne (10)   91
Katie McDonald (10)   91
Claire Brenchley (9)   92
Laura Robertson (10)   92
Hannah Thomson (9)   93
Corey Watt (10)   93
Ailsa Fraser (10)   93
Elspeth Wilson (9)   94
Callum Hancock (10)   94

Natasha Young (10)   95
Robert MacFarlane (9)   95
Samantha Bradley (10)   96
Leigh Chapman (9)   96
Nicola Henry (9)   97
Cameron Craig (9)   97
Rebecca Scoots (9)   97
Katherine Bryer (10)   98

Netherton Primary School, Wishaw
Kiah Taylor (11)   98
Adam Port (10)   99

Raploch Primary School, Stirling
Kimberley Wilson (7)   99
James Stewart (7)   100
Shannon Lafferty (8)   100
Sam Goodwillie (8)   100
Naomi McCallum (7)   101
Brooke Cameron (8)   101

Ravenscraig Primary School, Greenock
Andrew Cox (11)   101
Jamie Campbell (12)   102
Jordan Gostelow (11)   102
Karin Alexander (12)   103
David Nicholson (11)   103
Nicola Leith (11)   104

Rochsolloch Primary School, Airdrie
Ryan Clarke (10)   105
Zoe Shanks (10)   106
Nicole Middleton (10)   106
Ian MacPherson (10)   107
Heather Shea (11)   107
Josh Wallace (10)   108
Kerry Johnson (11)   109
Ailsa McRae (10)   110
Darren Pryde (10)   111
Ainsley Broadley (10)   112

St Andrew's RC Primary School, Gorebridge

Emma Laird (9)	112
Kelly McLeary (10)	113
Alana Hennessey (9)	113
Samantha Laing (10)	114
Andrew Knott (9)	114
Anne Hume (9)	115
Geordie Anderson (10)	115
Eilidh Yule (10)	115
Benjamin Allison (8)	116
Euan Richards (8)	116
Andrew Blair (9)	116
Nikki Clifford (9)	117
Jaydene Hamilton (9)	117
Claire McInally (8)	117
Shannon Allan (9)	118
Katey McGee (8)	118
Rosie Anderson (8)	119
Emily Brown (9)	119
Robyn Faughnan (8)	119
Becky McEwan (8)	120
Stuart Reid (9)	120
Daniel McConnell (8)	120
Sara Henderson (9)	121
Jack Fraser (8)	121
Jemma Henderson (9)	122
Louise Torrie (8)	122
Danielle Vass (10)	123
Matthew Allison (10)	123
Ty Hennessey (9)	124
Rachel Richardson (8)	124
Stephanie Napier (10)	125
Jed Baxter (9)	125
Jamie Doherty (10)	126
Ryan Russell (11)	126
Heather Lyon (9)	127
Lisa Loughrie (10)	127
Christopher Hogg (10)	128
Nathan Dalgleish (9)	128
Craig Tytler (10)	128
Rachel Napier (10)	129
Lauren Jardine (10)	129

St Peter's Primary School, Edinburgh

Matthew Duncan (9)	129
Gabriella Alonzi (10)	130
David Cooper (9)	130
Luke Paxton (10)	131
Stuart Brown (9)	131
Patrick Burns (9)	132
Tayla Garrod (10)	132
Thomas Gracie (10)	133
Maria Luisa Iannone (10)	133
Amber MacLeod (10)	134
Ross Muir (9)	134
Jamie Nicholson (9)	135
Joseph Flucker (7)	135
Ewan Feeney (12)	135
Geraldine Gray (9)	136
Michael Paterson (10)	136
Eilidh McMillan (10)	137
Daniel Pacitti (7)	137
Molly Donovan (7)	138
Matthew Gormley (7)	138
Anna Service (7)	138
Tom Jarvis (7)	139
Charlotte McGowan (7)	139
Adam Al Khateb (11)	139
Catrina Randall (11)	140
Eloise Cooper (7)	140
Anna Ghazal (11)	141
Lucia Corace (7)	141
Anya Macsorley Pringle (7)	142
Lesley Wong (10)	142
Matthew Gallagher (10)	143
Graham Goode (10)	143
Danielle Cathro (10)	144
Ruth Robertson (11)	144
William Reeves (11)	145
Blair Donaldson (11)	145
Emma McGachie (10)	146
Anne Cameron (10)	146
Sang Hee Lee (11)	146
Dominique Charleston (11)	147
Justin Hepburn (12)	147

Charlotte Dick (11)	148
Courtney Kyle (11)	148
Callum Kerr (10)	149
Daniela Cernicchiaro (10)	149
Sophie Dolan (11)	150
Ava Pullar (11)	150
Keira O'Sullivan Robertson (10)	151
Owen Mooney (10)	151
Hope Thompson (11)	152
Kealan Delaney (10)	152

Sciennes Primary School, Edinburgh

Morag Williams (10)	153
Kirstie-Ann McPherson & Rebecca Thomason (10)	153

Silverwood Primary School, Kilmarnock

Karis McKechnie (11)	154
Daniel King (12)	155
Darren Brown (12)	156
Emma-Lee Kelso (12)	156
Mikey Reynolds (11)	157
Jodie McMonagle (12)	158
Nicole Phillips (12)	159
Jason Murphy (11)	160
Stuart Johnstone (11)	161
Jodie Neilson (11)	162
Emma Rae (11)	163
Jennifer Wilson (12)	164
Gavin McLaughlin (11)	165
Aaron Graham (11)	166
Shelby Hollas (11)	167
Scott Jamieson (11)	168
Kari Todd (12)	169
Christopher Barbour (11)	170
Hannah McGill (12)	171

Stenhousemuir Primary School, Stenhousemuir

Eva Mitchell (9)	171
Mairi Mackellaig (8)	172
Chelcie MacKay (8)	172
Mychaela Mealey (8)	173

Graeme Wardrope (8)	173
Daniel Sharp (8)	174
Floyd Kesson (8)	174
Gary Grugen (8)	175
David Clark (8)	175
Ryan Miller (8)	175
Ashley Harrower (9)	176
Jack Mitchell (8)	176
Bronia Black (9)	177
Abbie Wishart (9)	177
Eva Brookes (8)	178
Callum Cochrane (8)	178
Jordan Thomson (8)	179
Caitlyn Blues (8)	179
Charlie Thomson (8)	180
Monica Caie (8)	180
Justin Laurie (8)	181
Keira Morrison (8)	181
Grant Robertson (8)	182

Tinto Primary School, Biggar

Chelsea Blacklaw (9)	182
Jenny Bruce (8)	182

Whitecross Primary School, Whitecross

Samantha Taylor (12)	183
Lorne Muldoon (11)	183
Jordan Braes (10)	183
Jason Miller (11)	184
Stacey Hunter (11)	184
Lisa McNeill (10)	184
Christopher Smith (11)	185
Jodie Dalglish (11)	185

The Poems

Seaside

Where could we go today?
On this lovely sunny day
We could go to the seaside,
The seaside and play!

Paddle in the water,
Or even go for a swim!
Have sandcastle competitions,
And see which one wins!

We could have a picnic,
On the shore
With juice, sweets,
Sandwiches and so much more!

I love the seaside,
It makes me smile,
It's sad this lovely weather,
Only lasts for a little while!

Debbie Cowley (11)
Annanhill Primary School, Kilmarnock

Goodbye

Thank you for my life so far,
but now it's time to go,
I do not want to do this,
Oh how I love you so.

You said he was not good for me,
That he was a waste of time,
You made me feel so bad about it,
That I felt it was a crime.

I know I'll have a good life,
Being with him all day,
And I'm sorry but if I like it,
I'm afraid I just might stay.

Lauren Strachan (11)
Annanhill Primary School, Kilmarnock

A Mouse's Tail

Once when I was a-building my house
I saw a little yellow mouse
I screamed to see the sight of it
I fainted to see the might of it
I got a cat
I called it Pat
But the cat was too fat
And it never killed the little yellow mouse
That lived in my a-building house
I got a trap
And with a tap
I got some cheese and a handful of peas
In a little pastry wrap
But the mouse was too clever
And it never fell for the trap
So I decided to be its friend
And got a couple of my pens
So together we sat
The mouse on my lap
And we wrote a poem and this is that!

Hayley Porter (10)
Annanhill Primary School, Kilmarnock

The Pig

'You really are a silly shape,'
They all said to the pig,
'Your beady eyes are much too small,
Your snout is much too big.
It is a mystery to us how you get up off the ground,
With all that blubber you insist,
On carrying around.'

'Your neck is hardly there at all,
You should hide it with a scarf.
Your tail is like a corkscrew,
And you have a stupid laugh.
It really is no wonder,
You are only fit for spam.'

The pig snorted from his muddy bed,
'I ham just what I ham!'

Mica Sinforiani (10)
Annanhill Primary School, Kilmarnock

The Battle

Over the horizon comes their boat
Sails up and ships afloat.
They'll stop their oar
And land on shore
Then the Vikings will wait for battle.
The Scottish men go for war
And leave their cattle,
They'll battle and bottle and bottle and battle
But none sees the cattle.
The cattle barge into the Vikings
The Vikings take their oar
And row away from our shore.

Jacob Keay (9)
Bruntsfield Primary School, Edinburgh

The Abandoned House

The window called me stupid today
Not very creative if I may say
He said 'I'm cleverer than you!'
I couldn't believe it, could you?

I wish I wasn't as lonely as a flower in a vase
With no one in the house
But a window and a mouse

The window called me idiotic a week ago
I ignored him and said 'So'
The window mocked 'You're so dim!
And also you are far too thin!'

I wish I wasn't as lonely as a flower in a vase
With no one in the house
But a window and a mouse

The window called me unfair
I really didn't care
The window cleaner came today - I didn't have a say
Then he washed the wickedness away.

Catriona James (9)
Bruntsfield Primary School, Edinburgh

Buzz . . . Buzz . . . Bumblebee!

Buzzing along
A little bumblebee
A little bumblebee called Pea
Today Pea was very happy
And collecting his pollen very snappy!
He was passing a lily
When he felt very silly
And went to read a book
He took a quick look
And saw a better book
A book from Bruntsfield library!

Isobel Filor (10)
Bruntsfield Primary School, Edinburgh

A Bad Day

When I went to school today
I thought the day would be okay
But when I went to maths
I thought it wouldn't last
Then soon my maths teacher got mad at me
As I was cheeky and calling her Miss B
I then got sent to the head teacher's room
I thought I was going to be doomed
She wrote a letter to my mum and dad
Saying I was being bad
After school I was on my way home
I felt like wanting to go on holiday to Rome
I knew I was going to be in big trouble from my mum
At that moment I felt numb
I was on the doorstep of my house
Oh I felt like a little mouse.

Sofina Begum (11)
Bruntsfield Primary School, Edinburgh

Spring Rap

Life is cool
Spring is here
The sun is shining
The lambs are here
The flowers are blooming
The blossom's out
And the baby rabbits, hopping about
Paint an egg
Roll it down a hill
Too much chocolate
Will make you ill!

Kay White (10)
Bruntsfield Primary School, Edinburgh

The Story Of Sophie Mate

This is the story of Sophie Mate,
who really liked to ice skate.
She was an extremely athletic girl,
could do a very, very good twirl.
So one day she went out to play,
and her mother had to say,
'Be careful, don't get hurt!
Don't mess up your lovely skirt.'
She said to her mum, 'Do not worry,
Let me go I'm in a hurry.'
So off she went with her friends,
round corners, twists and bends.
They arrived at the local ice rink,
to see the ice had turned bright pink,
and when it started to get dark,
out came a great white shark.
Sophie stood there really amazed,
all she did was stare and gaze,
and then the shark took his chance,
he said 'I'll take you, then go to France.'
So that's the story of Sophie Mate,
who really liked to ice skate,
but in the end came to a terrible fate.

Josh Platt (10)
Bruntsfield Primary School, Edinburgh

Billy The Slug

Meet ma pal Billy the slug
I think he's great but my mates think I'm a mug
'He canny dae anything,' they say
Get yoursel a proper pet like a cat or a dug.

Ma pal Billy is a slug,
He's much better than a cat or a dug!

Wi nae legs Billy's mainly head and tail,
An' he's easy to follow with his slimey trail!
He may no be as big as a whale,
But he always lets me hold him without fail!

Ma pal Billy is a slug
He's much better than a cat or a dug!

When I canny find him 'n think he's lost
I worry that he's been stood on 'n squashed
When I go hunting in the mud and the dirt
He's always there and never hurt.

Ma pal Billy is a slug,
He's much better than a cat or a dug!

One day Billy got stuck in a shell
'n how that happened a coudnae tell.
Maybe he'd had too much ale,
Who knows, but now I call him Sid the snail!

Amy Hood (11)
Bruntsfield Primary School, Edinburgh

Poems

I can't write a poem
It is impossible to write a poem
I am telling you it is true
So, what do you do to write a poem?
Just think of something
That you like to do
Then what do you do next?
You write it down in a poem
But how
Figure it out for yourself
Oh drat! Now what.

Zara Elmi (7)
Bruntsfield Primary School, Edinburgh

Looking Forward To 'Cats'

People excited for going to 'Cats'
wondering what it would be like
there,
Jumping about and crying with joy
even you would like it alot.
'Everyone why don't
you come?'
because if you do come
you will surely have lots of fun.
There's sly cats, silly cats
So come along
And have some fun,
because you will soon want to come
Again!

Gemma Rae (9)
Clachan Primary School, Tarbert

The Air Raid

Go to bed dreading death
dream of fires and fear
until the air raid siren goes
eeeeeeeeeeoooooowwww
you'll hear it cry
out you rush to the neglected night
where the platinum planes fly low
zoom, whizz, drone, they call through the dark
blasting bombs as they go
quick, quick, quick get in the shelter now
it's cold and damp but safe,
be fast, get in shut the door right now
bang, crash, weee the black bombs go
bang! It shouts out loud
now fire crackles right next door
flashing sparks appear
whilst flames in fury leap up high
a jet of water appears in answer
finally the fire's gone and we all go inside
a smile of relief passes over faces now we
all sleep.

Esther Stanesby (9)
Clachan Primary School, Tarbert

O They Be'er No Come Near!

I've just been ootside catching a moos
Just for the flamin' farmer so those *rogues*
do not eat his crops
Going up and doon the stair chasing them awa'
They be'er no come near or I will need to arrange to get
them a coffin
What a day it has been
Me gettin' shouted at just because they appear
O when I get me paws on them they will be sorry
O they be'er no come near!

Ashleigh Scarff (12)
Clachan Primary School, Tarbert

Bones: The Gangster Cat

Bones the gangster cat
is a deadly cat
he attacks the kittens
and steals their milk

He runs from the law
and he is called
the 'crabby claw'
he works with the best
of the bad
so do not try to stop
he just fights back

He is black with a white belly
and only has one eye
for attacking a dog
he lost part of his tail
so he has been trying
to get that dog caught down
but his try only leads him
down and down

He has never been caught
but one or two close calls
he has lost a few friends
but he never gets caught
he will never be caught
unless it is a dog.

Jamie Johnstone (11)
Clachan Primary School, Tarbert

Raiding

Sliding across the ocean
Racing with the tides
Return
Thanking Njord for
Good weather and
A safe crossing.

Beware, beware
Vikings are out to get you
Beware

Hair-raising faces
Gnashing teeth
Foul words
Terrifying eyes
Static hair
All rushing at you

Beware, beware
Vikings are out to get you
Beware

Screaming, crying
Wailing, howling
As *'charge'*
Is heard
Five hours later
Dead bodies. Silence.

Beware, beware
The Vikings have got you
Beware.

Katherine Duff (12)
Clachan Primary School, Tarbert

The Air Raid

Crash! The bomb blasting blackly came down.
The tapping of our feet trailing one after the other.
In the shelter shivering shaking in fear.
Hear the planes zooming across painted black.
We also hear the noise of the fire crackling flames things
are getting burnt.
People in the street crying in fear shouting, 'Help save me,'
I think to myself our city will be a mess.
Sitting with my gas mask on trying to think good thoughts.
The long siren goes it has finished we can go and see what
it has destroyed.
We go out and see a few dead people on the street,
they did not make it.

Lorna McCallum (10)
Clachan Primary School, Tarbert

Summer

Summer is fun, time to laugh and run
When you leave the door you'll be much more
Playing with friends means they will attend
Lots of things you do when they're out with you.

Jordan Ho (10)
Cleland Primary School, Cleland

Scotland

Scotland is a lovely place
Lots of different people to meet
All the fun things to do
Can I come and play with you?
Tablet is a yummy sweet
Shortbread is a traditional treat,
I like Scotland, I hope you do too.

Kirstie Robert (9)
Cleland Primary School, Cleland

My Dog

I was in the kitchen
Playing with my dog
And then I decided
To sing a rare bog

After I had sang the song
I took my dog for a run
At first it was very wet
But then out came the sun.

My dog is called Mandy
She is white
She runs about
And she is very bright.

Megan Currie (10)
Cleland Primary School, Cleland

Summer

S ummer is my favourite season
U nder blue skies
M e and my sister are playing a game
M y mum and dad are doing the gardening
E veryone is out in their garden
R emember to put on suncream.

Gillian Dorman (11)
Cleland Primary School, Cleland

Family And Friends

Family and friends are all you need
They will make you succeed
Family and friends are really happy
They will make you be happy as Larry
Family and friends are kind and helpful
They will be your guiding angel.

Ashley Scott (11)
Cleland Primary School, Cleland

The Match

Excitement
Excitement
Who's going to score?
This team, that team
It's the best feeling there
It's the goals that count
I love the waiting.

I love the unknown
But when they get into the box
I think I'll explode.
Excitement
Excitement.

Stuart Davies (10)
Cleland Primary School, Cleland

Clown

Here they come with custard pies,
Splat on your face surprise, surprise
The superb audience through the streets,
The people who you love to meet
They cycle around without no care
Having no notice to who is there
After that the circus fair.

Lauren Hattie (9)
Cleland Primary School, Cleland

Bonfire Night

Fireworks go *zoom,*
Then go *boom*
In the night-time gloom.
I shiver with fear then a tear.
Bonfire night is here.

Alexandra Gould (10)
Cleland Primary School, Cleland

Miss Cochrane

My teacher is called Miss Cochrane
She is beautiful, magnificent and smart
She has beautiful blonde shiny soft hair
And she loves strawberry tarts.

She has beautiful silky skin
Hazel-green eyes, rosy red lips,
She is brilliant, lovely, marvellous and bright
With her we love going on school trips.

Jacklyn Noble (9)
Cleland Primary School, Cleland

Summer

The wavy waves
The silky sand
Tells you that summer's here on this land
The shiny sun is everywhere,
It makes you want to stop and stare
The slimy seaweed
The glittery shells
The summer's sun is what I need.

Jessica Ho (9)
Cleland Primary School, Cleland

Unicorn

U nicorn, unicorn standing tall
N ever have you been outrun before
 I n every way you dazzle and shine,
C ouldn't have been a creature so fine.
O f all the ways I see you now,
R unning with your pearl white hooves,
    the white whooshing tail, the silver mane,
N ever will I be the same again.

Andrew Young (10)
Cleland Primary School, Cleland

School

School is fun, school is great, you are welcome
through our gate.
Never fear, we're always here,
Our teacher is very kind,
And she is always on our mind.
We are very smart at art,
I love maths it gives us laughs,
So that is our school,
And it makes us cool.

Ashley Napier (9)
Cleland Primary School, Cleland

Spring Is Here

Spring is here so fresh and new
As I look out in the morning I spot the glistening dew.
I hear the sweet birds in full song
Then it's off to school
As the school bell rings, *ding dong.*

Katie Stitt (10)
Cleland Primary School, Cleland

Friend

F riends are friendly
R ight and wrong
I reland they come from
E arly on
N ice to me like my family
D o you think they like to see me?

Kelsey Bannatyne (8)
Cleland Primary School, Cleland

My Senses

I can see a clown
I can see a crown
I can see a rainbow shining over town.

I can hear a hoot
I can hear a shoot
I can hear a car horn toot, toot, toot.

I can feel the sun
I can feel the moon
I can feel the stars above the moon.

I can smell the air
I can smell the care
I can smell the lightning in the air.

Tracey Fisher (10)
Cleland Primary School, Cleland

Sea

Dazzling dolphins everywhere,
People love to laugh and stare,
Everyone likes to lay in the sand
Wandering waves all around.
In the seashells hear that sound,
In the sea look on the ground,
Guess what you find? Look . . . a crab!
Down they lay on the slab.

Whooshing water,
Salty sea,
Come to the beach and you'll meet me!

Chloe Rose (9)
Cleland Primary School, Cleland

The Jungle

Down, down deep in the middle of the jungle
The swinging monkeys from tree to tree
The tumbling chimpanzees from palm trees
The lion is the king of the jungle
You will never believe that the jungle is a great place
With all the quiet things
With the tropical trees of the chimpanzees
The jungle is quite the place.

Alastair Leghorn (10)
Cleland Primary School, Cleland

Ssammy The Ssnake

Ssammy the ssnake
Is a sslimy ssnake
It sslitherss acrosss the floor
Ssammy the snake
Eatss lotss of thingss like
Gooey sslugs
Groovy mothss
Yummy frogss
That'sss what he likesss
And sso do I!

Alan Garden (10)
Cliftonhall School, Newbridge

The Chameleon

A n animal with a spark
B eautiful as a tiger
C rikey! Say his friends
D ring!
E ven . . .
F light-dwelling
G rabbers can't laugh at him.
H e hides to catch his prey.
I
J ust see it
K illing
L ots of insects
M mm . . .
N othing can
O ver-
P ower its
Q uick
R unning
S wift
T ongue
U nder leaves.
V ery
W eary and
X hausted
Y awn . . .
Z zzz . . .

Jamie Maclachlan (9)
Cliftonhall School, Newbridge

Snake

A mbushing its prey
B ig as an antelope
C runching its food
D anger to humans
E normous as can be
F ighting its way out of things
G ruesome to some people
H iding to catch its prey
I would stay back
J ust a big brute
K illing mammals
L unging
M unching
N o one can stand it
O ther animals beware
P ouncing
Q uickly as can be
R ustling through the rainforest
S wallowing its prey whole
T ight as can be
U nbeatable
V iolent
W et
X -ray skeleton
Y um- lunch!
Z ebra!

Thomas Short (9)
Cliftonhall School, Newbridge

The Chimpanzee

A crobatic
B lack
C himpanzees
D elightful
E njoying
F ruit
G orgeous
H airy
I tchy
J umping
K icking
L aughing
M onkey
N aughty
O rang-utan's cousin
P laying games
Q uiet
R estless
S inging
T icklish
U pside down
V ery clever
W inking
X ylophone
Y appy
Z ippy!

Alex-Jade Donaldson (9)
Cliftonhall School, Newbridge

The Parrot

A killer
B eak
C old black eyes
D eafening screech
E ntertaining
F emale
G rumpy
H ungry
I tching
J umping
K iller claws
L ounging around
M outh wide open
N othing to be found
O ops! Missed that
P recious bug
Q uick
R ough
S haking
T ouching
U nder vines
W ings flapping
X cratch
Y um
Z ip!

Donald Patrick (9)
Cliftonhall School, Newbridge

Sunset

The blowing breeze
Fades behind the trees
The fox comes out
There's something in the bushes with a long pointed snout.
The group of sparrows fly away
The hunting animals come out to play.
The hedgehogs sniff for wiggly snails
The slimy slugs leave their silver trails.
The bell strikes ten over the town
The fair packs away as the people laugh at the clown.
The fox tiptoes around
The moles stay underground.
The midges fly in the shadow
As the field mouse creeps in the meadow.
A jumpy, muddy frog
Jumps around in the forest's bog.
Creepy little insects huddle under the stone
While the pecky pigeons lick the last of an ice cream cone
The sun leaves a shiny glow in the water
As the little furry otter
Swims for its food and plays.
It will find its own little ways.
Dark fades behind the purple clouds and stays there all night long.
But when the morning rises, the church bell begins to sing a song.
But now we know what happens at night.
So there are no grizzly bears to give you a fright.
And when you hear a bird call in the morning hour
Lying hurt beside a flower
Feed it.
Just a little bit
Until it flies away.
You stand up to face the day
As it flows like a river
Never stops.
Again and again.
Till you know you're old
But this story will always be told.

Katie Matthews (10)
Cliftonhall School, Newbridge

Fishing

Fish
Got it
Thank you Lord

Lobster
Caught it
Thank you God

Salmon
Hooked it
Thank you Lord

Crab
Not got it
But thank you *Lord*.

Ariadne Weir (10)
Closeburn Primary School, Thornhill

Bruno

Bruno was a dog
He really liked the fog
He didn't like the sun
He didn't find it fun
So he prayed to God for fog
And became a happy dog!

Adele Queen (11)
Closeburn Primary School, Thornhill

Henrik Larsson Tanka

Larsson is so great
He is the best footballer
He plays for Celtic
He gives defenders a scare
He's my biggest role model.

Michael McAleavey (10)
Closeburn Primary School, Thornhill

Apples

Apples apples
They are so nice
They are crunchy
Juicy and sometimes are
A little sour.
So tuck right in and have a bite
They are so nice, I eat one every night
To keep me healthy
For a long time.

Callum Anderson (11)
Closeburn Primary School, Thornhill

Dogs

Vet haters
Food lovers
Furry friends
Mucky pups
Cat chasers
Fence jumpers
Toy lovers
Loud barkers.

Dale McGenily (11)
Closeburn Primary School, Thornhill

Holidays

Holidays are the best
You can go from east to west
You can have a lot of fun
Playing in the afternoon sun
Holidays are never pests
They give you a chance for rests.

Catherine Moodycliffe (10)
Closeburn Primary School, Thornhill

Charlie's Cat

Charlie Clifford had a cat
It chased mice and things like that
It always stole Charlie's seat
And would not eat his normal meat.
Then one day things did change
When Charlie went to a rifle range.
The cat was scared of his gun
While Charlie, he had lots of fun.
The cat decided it would be good,
For Charlie's sake he thought he should.

Maimie Sloan (10)
Closeburn Primary School, Thornhill

My Little Brother

My little brother is a maniac
He swings on the shelves
He rides on the cat.

He really doesn't know when to stop
He keeps on going
All through the day and night.

When he goes over the top
Dad stops him
With a smack on the bot.

David Kennedy (11)
Closeburn Primary School, Thornhill

Favourites - Haiku

I quite like tractors
Tractors are quite tremendous
I hope to drive one.

Matthew McMillan (9)
Closeburn Primary School, Thornhill

Favourite Things!

Winter, summer, autumn, spring
these are some of my favourite things.
Swimming, tap, things like that
I like lots of wedding hats.
Gems, rocks,
I've got quite a stock.
Animals, friends
I've got lots of them.

Grace Dale (9)
Closeburn Primary School, Thornhill

Rabbit

Carrot muncher
Radish cruncher
Foot stomper
Happy chomper
Burrow digger
Hutch liver
Lettuce chewer
Happy hopper.

Elisha Scott (10)
Closeburn Primary School, Thornhill

Favourite Things

Opening presents
Playing cards
Yummy fruits
Singing songs
Playing music
Rainbow colours
Silver chains
Favourite things.

Ariane Porter (10)
Closeburn Primary School, Thornhill

Music

Music, happy, romantic or sad
Sometimes good and sometimes bad
Violins, flutes and recorders
Lots of music comes from orchestras
Music, peaceful, noisy or fast
Sometimes played like a blast
Pianos, drums and clarinets
Sometimes even castanets!
Music loud, music clear,
It is all I want to hear.
Saxophones, bells and violas
I like music from all over.

Emily Count-Stewart (10)
Closeburn Primary School, Thornhill

Children

Children in the classroom
Children out to play
Children out everywhere
They're there night and day.

Children buying sweets
They eat more and more
Growing every day
Until they can't fit through the door!

Samantha Keene (11)
Closeburn Primary School, Thornhill

A Dog - Haiku

Dogs love food to eat
Dogs like to bark in the night
Lots of cats hate dogs.

Jack Howat (9)
Closeburn Primary School, Thornhill

My Hat And Brolly!

My hat I wear on sunny days
It holds so many memories
Of playing loads and having fun
My hat is loved by everyone!

But when it then begins to rain
My brolly it comes out again
It keeps me cosy, nice and dry
If I lost it I would cry!

Alice Findlater (11)
Closeburn Primary School, Thornhill

Friends!

My friends are like family
I thought I knew them inside out,
Until I noticed they liked Katie
A lot, lot more than me.
It left me feeling low and sad
Until I met another friend
That left me with no doubt!

Kirsty Clark (11)
Closeburn Primary School, Thornhill

Mouse

Cheese nibbler
Owl's victim
Playmate
Creepy treader
Scary creature
Fast runner
Cat's dinner

Loren Rammell (12)
Closeburn Primary School, Thornhill

A Lifetime

At first you're born
Upon this planet
This big, bright light,
My gosh what is it?

Soon school has come,
Your very first day
Out at play time,
All you do is play.

Now you're grown up,
And all big and tall,
Married you are,
With kids very small.

Now you are old,
And empty of might
Lying in bed
Again you see light.

Michael Blunsden (11)
Closeburn Primary School, Thornhill

Summer Day

The colourful butterflies drift and flutter away
on the hot summer's day.

The playful children splash and play in their
paddling pools.

The harmful bees fly away into the blue
fluffy sky.

The ice cream man comes on the hot summer day
with a cool ice cream.

The ladies sunbathe in the hot days
of the year trying to get a tan.

Lynsey Keegan
Craigour Park Primary School, Edinburgh

Down At The Beach On A Summer's Day

Shiny, crashing, roaring waves race to the soft and sandy shore.

The blinding, hissing, sizzling sun, sheds heat and light
upon everyone having fun.

Ice cream van sings his loud noisy song while everybody
joins along.

Children slurping on their lovely freezing ice cream cones,
while others jump the glittering waves.

A smiling, playful, non-stop dog rapidly swims to get his ball
before the waves drag it out to sea.

The children are puzzled of what the shape shifting clouds
might be.

Gemma Bartie (11)
Craigour Park Primary School, Edinburgh

Summer's Day

The twirling sounds of the ice cream van rolling to a gentle stop
and roaring children rushing to get their delicious ice cream.

The chirping and singing of delightful birds
and their new chicks crying for food.

The glistening sun shooting through the air as the shining heat
bounces off cars and trucks.

The bright yellow sand burning people's feet and the
glittering blue sea.

The loud children happily playing in the parks and fields.

Nuts are gathered as the squirrels rushing to get all the nuts
to wave the summer goodbye.

Paul McGinnity (11)
Craigour Park Primary School, Edinburgh

Summer's Day

Sparkling, glittery, shiny ocean gliding across the earth and with slippery, beautiful, intelligent fish who are going along with it.

Tiny, little hardworking ant carrying a leaf to its dark, greasy mucky nest.

Overheated, water-thirsty people playing games in the breathtaking, magnificent and non-stop playing park.

The calm, smooth, relaxing wind soars across the sky with the unstoppable, outraging, sun guiding the way.

A playful, delightful, smiling dog catching an old, bitten slobbery frisby.

The outstanding, vast dazzling sky with the white, fluffy calming clouds which blew the strong air away.

Brett Clayton (10)
Craigour Park Primary School, Edinburgh

Summer's Day

Laughing, loud, playful children playing with their coloured bikes.

Bright, relaxing, sleepy birds having their baby birds.

Soft, gentle, coloured red, pink, white and blue fresh flowers.

Furry, playful dog running through the magnificent sun.

Colourful, shiny, smooth butterfly fluttering around in the blue sky.

Small red, black, spotted ladybirds walking on the glittering ground and some in the bright blue sky.

Tara Blackley (10)
Craigour Park Primary School, Edinburgh

Summer's Day

The birds all singing songs, newborn babies crying for food,
Mothers chirping as their new babies warble.

The sun's magnificent, powerful, glittering rays are blindingly
hot.

The playful, slobbering, furry, cute puppy lying on the mat beside the
fire.

The gorgeous smell of the blood red plant.

The soft mucky grass growing and glittering after the football's
finished.

The calm and relaxing people playing in the shining sun.

Paul Grant (10)
Craigour Park Primary School, Edinburgh

What A Fib Poem!

'*Kurtis* it is well past your bedtime
hurry up and switch off your PlayStation'
'Mum I am too scared.'

'Kurtis you need to hurry up
And switch it off
Is there a spider on top of it?'
'Mum I am too scared.'

'Do you know how to switch it off?
Kurtis switch it off at the plug'
'Mum I am too scared
There is a werewolf on my TV
And a sniper behind my chest of drawers.'

Kurtis McLeod (12)
Crawforddyke Primary School, Carluke

Whit A Fib

'Marc hurry up and get to your bed!'
'But Mum it isn't possible!'
'Are the covers too dirty?
Well if they are go into my room
and get another pair.'
'But Mum it isn't possible.'
'Are the springs sticking out?
If it is flip it over, but hurry up.'
'But Mum, it isn't possible!
There's a herd of pink killer penguins
and they've just eaten my bed!'

Marc Muir (11)
Crawforddyke Primary School, Carluke

No Can Do!

'Vicky please go and hang the washing out!'
'Sorry no can do!'
'Can you not find your shoes to go outside in?
You can borrow mine for a minute.'
'Sorry Mum! *No Can Do!*'
'*Oh* I get it you're jam packed with homework! Well why don't
you do your homework once you've hung the clothes *out!*'
'I said *no can do!* There are hungry gorillas swinging from the
washing line with *knives!*'

Vicky Cumming (12)
Crawforddyke Primary School, Carluke

Dogs

D almations are so cute
O ther dogs are too
G reyhounds are so sweet
S weet like sugar.

Adele Johnston & Melissa Brownlee (11)
Crawforddyke Primary School, Carluke

Adding Poem

When I do maths I am as bright as the sun,
Adding together, what's one plus one?'
Maths is the thing that I like to do,
Adding together, what's two plus two?
Maths is the thing that I like to see,
Adding together, what's three plus three?
Maths starts when I open the door,
Adding together, what's four plus four?
When I do maths I feel so alive,
Adding together, what's five plus five?
Maths is the problem solving I have to fix,
Adding together, what's six plus six?
Easy maths stops when you're eleven,
Adding together, what's seven plus seven?
When I do maths I feel really great,
Adding together, what's eight plus eight?
When I do maths the joy is mine,
Adding together, what's nine plus nine?
Now I can do maths with a pen,
Adding together, what's ten plus ten?

Hannah Thomson (8)
Crawforddyke Primary School, Carluke

Recycling

R emember to put your rubbish in a recycling bin
E veryone is trying so should you
C ool kids collect cans to be recycled
Y ou can help the environment by recycling
C aring about the planet
L earn how to treat the planet
E verybody recycle cans, crisp bags etc.

Kerry Reid (11)
Crawforddyke Primary School, Carluke

Horses!

Horses come in all different colours:
Black, brown, bay,
And you might think there's a white horse
When actually it's grey!

Horses come in different sizes:
Large, medium, small
Some horses can be eighteen hands
Which is very, very tall!

I love horses they're so cool
I think that they're the best
They're my favourite animals
They're better than the rest!

Eilidh Carmichael (12) & Stephanie Walker (11)
Crawforddyke Primary School, Carluke

Five Little Romans

Five little Romans fighting in a war,
One dropped dead and then there were four.
Four little Romans bashing down a tree,
One hurt himself and then there were three.
Three little Romans tying their shoes,
One couldn't tie and then there were two.
Two little Romans sitting in the sun,
One got burnt and then there was one.
One little Roman standing on his own,
He couldn't win a war so he went back to Rome.

Hannah Robertson (8)
Crawforddyke Primary School, Carluke

I Wanna Be

I wanna be a popstar,
who shines in the light
I wanna dance my heart out,
All through the night.

I wanna be an author,
Who writes loads of stories
Who writes non-fiction fairytales,
And lots of gruesome gories.

I wanna be a director,
And boss around all the stars
Telling them where to sit,
In their brand new swanky cars.

I wanna be a doctor
With all the guts and blood
I wanna save loads of lives,
Of people who were in a flood.

I wanna be in the West End,
And show them who to sing
I wanna play a brilliant part,
And wear a diamond ring!

I wanna be a teacher,
And teach the little children
I wanna read them loads of books,
I'd nearly earn a million.

No I don't think these jobs
Are what I want to be
I'd rather just be plain and simple,
And just be *me!*

Lisa Rattray (12)
Crawforddyke Primary School, Carluke

Raking The Garden

'Scott hurry up and rake that garden.'
'Maw, I canny.'
'Why, is the rake broken? If it is use the broom then,
but hurry it up.'
'Maw, I canny.'
'Why is there no black bin liners? Use some Safeway bags
then but hurry up and start raking!'
'Maw I canny!'
'There's a vicious dog with rabies waiting to bite the next
person to walk into the garden.'

Scott Melvin (11)
Crawforddyke Primary School, Carluke

Turn Off The Computer

'Ashley hurry up and turn off the computer.'
'Mother I can't.'
'Have you crashed it?
Try to restart it.'

'Mother I can't'
'Do you know how to turn it off?
Use the button on the front of the computer.'
'Mother I can't
There is a big enormous dog sitting on it and it has
just eaten it.'

Ashley Wigston (11)
Crawforddyke Primary School, Carluke

What A Fib

'Kirsten can you wash the dishes for me?'
'Mum I can't.'
'Is there not enough Fairy left in the tube?
Just go in the cupboard there is another one there.'
'Mum I can't.'
'Is the water too hot?
Just put in some cold but
get on with it.'
'Mum I can't.
There's an alien it came up the plug hole and I
think it's taking me down with it.'

Kirsten Stuart (11)
Crawforddyke Primary School, Carluke

What A Fib

'Shari go and put your clothes in the cupboard.'
'Mum I can't.'
'Has your shelves fallen down?
Because if they have you know how to put them back up
but move a little faster.'
'Mum I can't.'
'Have your clothes unfolded?
If they have then fold them again but hurry up.'
'Mum I can't.
There are gremlins in the cupboard and they are
playing fancy dress and I think they are going to fancy dress
me in a minute and it does not look very pretty.'

Shari Nicol (12)
Crawforddyke Primary School, Carluke

Sunny Day

Sizzling hot sun sits in the sky
Birds flying high, high, high.
Burning sun in your face
Bees and wasps flying about the place
Butterflies flying in the gentle breeze
The sizzling hot sun
It's a bundle of fun
So just enjoy the day
It will be gone soon anyway.

Rebecca McGuire (11)
Cumbernauld Primary School, Cumbernauld

Hickory Dickory

Hickory dickory hot
The sun is sizzling hot
Hickory dickory dong
The birds are singing a song
Hickory dickory paces
There's so many smiling faces
Hickory dickory bareoke
The bees are buzzing in a karaoke.

Adam Smith (11)
Cumbernauld Primary School, Cumbernauld

A Sizzling Hot Day

Sizzling hot sun with candyfloss clouds
Bees buzzing to the hummingbird sound
The aqua blue sky and the birds flying high.

Blinding sun
Butterflies flapping their wings
Lovely colours to see
Children playing having fun.

Dionne Wilson (10)
Cumbernauld Primary School, Cumbernauld

Hot Day

It's a very hot day
And the birds are squawking
There is a breeze
And people are talking

Buzzing bees are in the air
All I can feel is a red-hot flair
Melting clouds fading away
Like a melting candy-spray

Butterflies with smiley faces
While the children tie their laces
Birds are tweeting while they fly
No clouds are in the sky.
Goodbye.

Ryan Dynes (10)
Cumbernauld Primary School, Cumbernauld

A Sunny Day

Shining sun is so fun
Makes me want to smile
Every time I see the sun
I just want to have a little fun.

You see little bumblebees
Buzzing in the trees
Oh the sun, the sun,
Is such fun.

The sun makes my day
I don't want it to go away
When it turns dark at night
I just want to have sunlight.

Susannah Beattie (11)
Cumbernauld Primary School, Cumbernauld

The Sun

The sun is sizzling
The sun is burning
The sun is making people smile
The sun is burning clouds away
The sun is making the sky sparkle
The sun is making people travel
The sun is making people melt
The sun is making mountains shine
The sun is melting the world
The sun made the world bright.

Jordan Stewart (11)
Cumbernauld Primary School, Cumbernauld

Sunny Poem

I saw the candyfloss clouds
I saw the birds tweeting
I saw the butterflies flapping their wings
I saw the children with happy faces
I saw the baby blue skies
I saw the bees buzzing
I saw the blinding sun.

I saw the sunny sun!

Aimeé Pollock (11)
Cumbernauld Primary School, Cumbernauld

Sunny

S izzling sun in the baby blue sky
U nhappy faces when it is raining
N ice happy faces when it is sunny
N ice big bright sun in the sky
Y ummy big doughnuts.

Eilish Barrett (11)
Cumbernauld Primary School, Cumbernauld

The Sun In The Sky

The sun in the sky
The birds squawking
The clouds are like candyfloss
The birds are flying
The sun is smiling
The clouds are crying with happiness
The sun is sizzling
The kids are having ice cream
It's very warm.

Scott McFaulds (11)
Cumbernauld Primary School, Cumbernauld

Sizzling Hot Sun

Sizzling hot sun sitting in the sky
Birds flying high, high in the sky
Smiling faces all around the world
Butterflies flying all around
Bees buzzing in the fiery sun
Birds squawking through the candyfloss clouds
Rabbits running through the shiny green grass

The sun is so much fun!

Siobhan Black (10)
Cumbernauld Primary School, Cumbernauld

Sunny Days

The sun shining away
What a beautiful day
Birds squawking in the sun
I feel happy, no time to run
The sun shining up in the sky
I wish I could fly.

Euan Calder (10)
Cumbernauld Primary School, Cumbernauld

The Sunny Days

Sunny days are so great
Smiling faces all around
Birds squawking in trees
Sizzling hot May in time.

Rainy days are so bad
But when it's sunny I'm glad
People playing all around
Sizzling hot May in time.

Sunny days are so great
There's a sunny day coming
Watch the sky form so great
Sizzling hot May in time.

Johnathon Yau (10)
Cumbernauld Primary School, Cumbernauld

The Sun

The sun's sparkling
The sun's cracking
The sun's shining

The sun's bright
The sun is sparkling

The sun's sparkling
The sun's cracking
The sun's shining.

The sun is cracking
The sun is shining.

Gary Love (11)
Cumbernauld Primary School, Cumbernauld

Snow

The white untouched snow lies like a soft blanket of
pearls upon the ground
It lies crisp and crunching,
Waiting to be trodden on.

White flakes of snow fall upon bare windows and sills
Making them whiter and whiter
Making them like a table covered by a soft, white lace
cloth.

The children come out and their angels lie in the snow,
Waiting to be covered by the next white blanket to fall
upon the ground.

Samantha Little (11)
Cumbernauld Primary School, Cumbernauld

Blizzard

The boy in the street frozen solid
The snow howling, drops of snow as big as
Hedgehogs, falling from the sky.

Snow pouring out of the sky, thump, thump
Thump, that's all you can hear in your bed
When trying to get asleep.

The next morning all is calm and out
Of the window all is white, the tree like
A giant polar bear sitting in the garden.

A blank world.

Andrew Mooney (11)
Cumbernauld Primary School, Cumbernauld

Sun Days Poem

The candyfloss clouds are sitting proud
The blinding sun is cooking my skin.

Birds are squawking everywhere
Butterflies flying here and there.

Everyone smiling here and there
Everyone smiling everywhere
Everyone keeping their cool
Everyone tanning and having fun
Everyone is here to stay
Everyone is outside to play
The sun is here to stay.

Andrew MacQueen (10)
Cumbernauld Primary School, Cumbernauld

A Hot Day

The sun beams down all around
As the black clouds fade away
To make a lovely sunny day.

A hot day is here today
So don't waste it
Buy some candyfloss
Play in the park.

I know what you have to do today
You're going to enjoy the sun,
Before this lovely sunny day,
Starts to fade away.

Emma Sommerville (10)
Cumbernauld Primary School, Cumbernauld

The Listeners And Silver

(Inspired by 'The Listeners' by Walter De La Mare.)

The traveller galloped away on his horse
Riding towards the town
While Aunt Marie opened the door
Dressed in her nightgown.
'Who's there?' she called out
Her voice echoing in the sky
But nobody came riding back
To answer her whimpering cry.
So to bed, she hopped up the stairs
To rest and to dream,
And in the morning she would eat
Some strawberries and cream.
Thinking about food she fell asleep
Dreaming about apple pie
Until the sun rose and travelled up
Lighting the blue sky.
The listeners are nightmares
Prying in dark nights,
And so the light, as you can guess
Gave them quite a fright!
They scarpered here and there
Away to visit a friend,
And so with this last line
Comes our story to an end!

Lauren Pickering (12)
Cumbernauld Primary School, Cumbernauld

Sunny Poem

S unny sky
U nbeautiful clouds are playing
N ever ever see funny clouds
N ever see the sun smile
Y ellow birds are smiling.

Tom Robertson (11)
Cumbernauld Primary School, Cumbernauld

Thunderstorm

Cloud like a sheet of blackness
covering everything. Thunder rumbles
and grumbles like an angry dog.
Lightning flashes like a huge torch
lighting everything up.
Rain pouring down like bullets
flooding roads and fields.
The wind rages like a bull charging,
hail batters down, denting cars
and smashing windows.

Anthony Morgan (12)
Cumbernauld Primary School, Cumbernauld

Hailstones

Hailstones are like crashing pearls
from the sky.
Everything is miserable.
The sky is grey and no animals are out.
The birds are not in flight.

Scott Greenlees (11)
Cumbernauld Primary School, Cumbernauld

April Rain

It starts when the big black clouds burst,
Dampening people's moods and making
them miserable.
Everywhere and everything is wet,
But when it finishes, it leaves a fresh, April
smell.

Rebecca Wilson (12)
Cumbernauld Primary School, Cumbernauld

Rainforest

Trees as tall as giants stretching up and up
A big white blanket of heat covers the trees
Parrots screaming and squawking
As colourful as a rainbow
Gliding through the branches
An army of marching armadillos
Mad monkeys crazy for food
Crawling centipedes creeping through the jungle
The rain falls down and the steam rises up
That's the way the rainforest grows.

Grant Kilby (10)
Drumlemble Primary School, Campbeltown

Rainforest

A city of giant trees reaching up to the sky
An enormous tribe of green camouflaging the forest floor
Mad monkeys doing a jungle dance high up in the canopies
Multicoloured frogs leaping from lily pad to lily pad
Rain falls down, steam floats up
The rainforest is a mysterious place.

Scott Anderson (10)
Drumlemble Primary School, Campbeltown

The Rainforest

A gang of long giant trees
A scraping haven of green
Arrow-poison frogs hunt for food
Sluggish sloths sleep all day
Mad monkeys swing from tree to tree
Tropical rain drizzles onto the forest floor
As the hot steam rises up
The rainforest it will always be.

Christopher Lang (10)
Drumlemble Primary School, Campbeltown

Rainforest

Monkeys swing from branch to branch
Vines like a rope over a wide blue river
Coconut trees as high as the biggest skyscraper
Tropical birds squawking all day long
In bushes as green as olives
Cobras slither across the forest floor
As the rain falls down.

Greg Newlands (10)
Drumlemble Primary School, Campbeltown

Rainforest

A mob of green giants
Like a big bunch of broccoli
Prowling leopards searching for
their prey
Monkeys practising their jungle
dance
Slow motioned sloths climbing the trees
Rain splashes down
Steam floats up
The rainforest comes alive.

David Crawford (11)
Drumlemble Primary School, Campbeltown

The Rainforest

A tribe of green trees supporting each other
Like giant crane reaching the sky
Mad monkeys swinging a crazy jungle dance
Lazy leopards lying looking for lunch
Slithering snakes slinking through the grass
Strong armadillos patrolling the forest
The rainforest never sleeps.

Graeme McMillan (10)
Drumlemble Primary School, Campbeltown

The Rainforest

The trees are as tall as lamp posts in the street
They cover the ground with their long leaves
Colourful birds fly in and out of giant trees
The spotty leopards are looking for their prey
Energetic frogs hop, hop, hopping on the ground
The rain is falling
Splish, splash, splashing
That's your tropical rainforest.

Lindsey Armour (9)
Drumlemble Primary School, Campbeltown

The Rainforest

An army of trees
All different shades of leaves
Leaping leopards pouncing around
Armadillos scuttling across the ground
Monkeys swinging to and fro
There goes a snake slithering below
Rain that falls looks like crying
The rainforest is never dying!

Jennifer Kelly (10)
Drumlemble Primary School, Campbeltown

The Rainforest

A gathering of giant trees
Different shades of green leaves
Slow sloths climbing on branches
Mad monkeys swinging from tree to tree
Slithery snakes searching on the ground
The rain splashes gently as it hits the ground
Hunting leopards finding their prey
The rainforest will never die.

Ben Craig (10)
Drumlemble Primary School, Campbeltown

The Rainforest

Trees here, trees there
Rainforest trees
A skyscraping haven of green
Red, blue, yellow and green flashes
Are seen flitting from branch to branch
Macaws come squawking
Everything's awoken
Hissing, slithering snakes searching for a snack
Hunting leopards, dangerous to meet
But soon it will be night
Then silent and swift, the bats will come swooping
Down through the trees
The rainforest as it should be.

Andrew McClement (9)
Drumlemble Primary School, Campbeltown

The End

A desert of abandoned trees
Miles of dead stumps
No living thing will ever walk
On that ground again
Very lonely
Alone and sad
Very, quiet and silent
Nothing left to destroy
It's the end of the rainforest as we know it.

Catherine Armour (11)
Drumlemble Primary School, Campbeltown

The Rainforest

An army of trees swaying with the wind
Leaves in green, yellow and red
Armoured armadillos sucking up ants
Like a powerful hoover
Monkeys doing the jungle dance
In the green leafy trees
Colourful parrots squawking on almost
Every branch
People underneath talking in a strange language
Fiery hot sun beating down below
Pitter-patter goes the rain
On nearly every leaf and tree
The rainforest is almost the same every day.

Lorna Armour (11)
Drumlemble Primary School, Campbeltown

Rainforest

Crowds of giant green verdant trees
towering high above the ground
Colourful parrots squawking all round
Multicoloured frogs hopping around
Armadillos showing off their plates of armour
Slithering snakes sliding through the olive grass
The rain comes pattering down onto the
sparkling emerald green leaves
The rainforest will never die.

James Cairns (9)
Drumlemble Primary School, Campbeltown

Wipe Out

An abandoned wildlife centre
Suffocated in burning fire
A great habitat destroyed
An army of the dead
A forest of nothing
Like a graveyard, the tree stumps as
gravestones
Wreckage raining
At the end of the rainforest there is no
pot of gold.

Adam Bellamy (11)
Drumlemble Primary School, Campbeltown

The Rainforest

A huge tribe of trees
A city of skyscraping green
Jerky frogs jump around
Flittery butterflies fly up and down
in and out the trees
Slow sloths sleep all day
Little fluff insects looking like candyfloss
Crawling on the forest floor
The rain slides off the shiny, slippery leaves
The forest will never die.

Eilidh Gaughan (9)
Drumlemble Primary School, Campbeltown

The Rainforest

A flowing river of giant, green trees
Leathery plants standing proudly
Wild baboons leaping from vine to vine
Mad monkeys practising a jungle dance
Poisonous slippery snakes slithering round the trees
Unhurried sloths sleep through the day
Slimy multicoloured frogs hopping along the forest floor
That's a day in the rainforest.

Louise Mitchell (10)
Drumlemble Primary School, Campbeltown

The Rainforest

Tall giant trees covering the ground
Green, lime, olive, emerald leaves create a canopy of shade
Slow sloths sleeping most of the day
Brown and green striped snakes slithering along the ground
Multicoloured parrots squawking up in the sky
Mad monkeys swinging branch to branch
The rain pitter-patters gently onto the leaves
The rainforest will always be the same.

Alison Millar (10)
Drumlemble Primary School, Campbeltown

The Rainforest

A crowd of thin trees
Mad monkeys jumping up and down
Colourful parrots flying in the sky
Different coloured pointy leaves
Slithering snakes slink through the forest
Slimy frogs jumping on each lily pad
Creepy crawlies scampering across the ground
The rainforest will always live.

Tiffany Lang (8)
Drumlemble Primary School, Campbeltown

Dead

A great habitat destroyed
Drowned in fire
A forest of nothing
Left to rot
The tribe of trees has been invaded
Leaving miles of dead rotten wood
An abandoned wildlife centre
At the end of the rainforest
There is no pot of gold.

Kerr Gaughan (11)
Drumlemble Primary School, Campbeltown

Peek Through The Window

Peek through the window
Maybe outside, maybe there is a sunset,
Or a shining star shining bright,
Or a full moon.

Peek through the window
There might be a rainbow,
Or a winding gold shining path,
Or a large pot of gold.

Peek through the window
Maybe there are happy voices, smiles and people shouting hello
Or bags of laughter
Or falling tears of joy.

Peek through the window
Maybe there is someone who is crying for your help
An outstretched hand waiting to be grabbed
Or a lonely face looking for company.

Peek through the window
What do you see?
What do you want to see?
Do you see yourself?
Or someone in danger?

Lauren Ward (10)
Drummore Primary School, Stranraer

Stare Through The Window

Stare through the window
Maybe outside there is a lovely sunset
Or a shining gold star
Or a full silvery moon.

Stare through the window
Maybe there is a multicoloured
Rainbow and a winding long golden path
And a secure pot of gold.

Stare through the window
Maybe there are happy and cheeky
Voices and smiles
Or bays of laughter
Or a rain fall of tears.

Stare through the window
Maybe there is someone who desperately
Needs you
An outstretched hand
Or a lonely and sad face.

Stare through the window
What do you see?
Who do you see?

Shaun Slavin (10)
Drummore Primary School, Stranraer

The Song Of The Leopard

Mighty queen of the jungle is stalking its prey
They never saw you
Hunting
You're ruthless and sinful
It's dead.

Back at the palace the cubs are waiting
They see you
Feasting
You're loving and caring
They eat.

The men are calling out and shooting
They saw you
Eating
You're scared and worried
You fall

They do not care about the cubs
They saw them
Weeping
They're mad and cruel
They're happy.

Scott Hose (11)
Drummore Primary School, Stranraer

The Song Of The Tiger

In the grassy plains of the quiet Savannah,
Tiger, I heard you
Weeping.

Standing tall and frightened,
Like mountains shaking after
An earthquake.

How we use your kind,
Your stripy fur coats for fashion,
Wealthy couples buy tiger rugs.

The Chinese use you for medicine,
To heal their patients.

Leaping tiger in the wild,
Running for your life,
Tiger I saw you,
Crying.

Tiger, I sense you know your fate,
I'm sorry.

The sound of the gun,
Bullets of pain.

Tiger,
I'm sorry.

Kara Torrance (12)
Drummore Primary School, Stranraer

What Is the Moon?

A white wide weary face
In the darkness,
Staring down at us,
The peaceful Earth
Spinning round and round, calmly.

A beautiful bronze button,
Sewn onto
The black coat
Of night.

An enormous eyebrow,
Hanging in the sky,
That's raised up into a
Question.

A bright ball
Floating high,
Edged in silver.

Jennifer McClintick (10)
Drummore Primary School, Stranraer

It Wisnae Me!

Somewhere on my bedroom floor,
Lies the carpet I've never seen before,
Clothes and junk are all you see,
I'm telling you Mum it wisnae me!

Toys are blocking the living room door,
The juice stain is on the floor,
Half-eaten biscuits on the settee,
Believe me Mum it wisnae me!

Rebecca MacPherson (9)
Dalintober Primary School, Campbeltown

Big Top

Clowns are there,
Some in the air,
Flying high above,
Come to the circus,
Come to the circus,
At the Big Top.

Lions are there
None in the air
None flying high above
Come to the circus,
Come to the circus,
At the Big Top.

Kerry McDougall (11)
Dalintober Primary School, Campbeltown

On My Day Away To Stranraer And Back!

I went to Stranraer to spend my pocket money,
It was too far so it wasn't very funny.

We came to a farm full of Hereford cattle,
We drove up the road and the car went rattle, rattle.

I looked through the herd and saw my Heather
My mum and the farmer had a very long bleather.

I got Heather, my sister got Holly,
We loaded them up like they were on a shopping trolley.

When we got home we put them into a pen
Now Heather weighs the same as three men.

But that was about three years ago,
Believe you me my sister would know.

They are expecting any day
I hope they will always forever stay!

Gavin Dunbar (11)
Gilmourton Primary School, Strathaven

My First Sail

This is the story
Of my first sail
I thought it would be scary
But I didn't go pale

When we stepped onto the dock
I had a look round
I walked straight past the boat
And then I turned round

When we got started
I got to steer the boat
When it started rocking
I thought it wouldn't float

When we got back to the dock
I felt really sad
And when we got on
I thought it would be bad

Now you've heard my story
What do you think?
Now that I've told it
I'm starting to go pink!

Jill Naismith (9)
Gilmourton Primary School, Strathaven

The Fairy Dance

A single fairy flies gracefully into the old trunk of a tree,
The spring flowers sway gently in the invisible breeze,
Everything is quiet, until the moon shines down on the trees,
The sliver light, awakening the fairies,
The fairies fly delicately to where a single beam of moonlight shines,
Two fairies, a handsome man and a beautiful woman dance,
They dance a slow magical dance, that tells a story,
A story about the two people who danced the magical fairy dance.

Rhiah McLean (10)
Gilmourton Primary School, Strathaven

Saturday Night Fever

Saturday night fever's got a hold
On everybody, weak or bold.
Sleepovers in full swing,
Gangsters about saying 'I'm the king!'
Late night movies on the box
Girls playing with golden locks.

Saturday night fever's got a hold,
On everybody, warm or cold.
Ships are swaying in the dock,
Crabs and fish are having a talk.
Sea is swaying to and fro,
Tides are changing, high and low.

Saturday night fever's got a hold,
On all the girls who have been told,
Blue is playing underground,
The noise can be heard from all around
Boys are at the football game,
They would take a war to tame!

Saturday night fever's got a hold,
On everybody, young or old,
Grannies, grandpas, playing cards,
Cars are parked out in the yards.
All us kids are all in bed,
So to rest our sleepy heads.

Rachel Naismith (11)
Gilmourton Primary School, Strathaven

The Snake

I was eating a cake and I saw a snake,
It was tangled up and it looked stuck.
So I called the vet and he said he was wet.
But he came down and he frowned.
He said it was risky and he needed some whisky,
It melted the wire and the snake was free.

Martin Cowan (10)
Gilmourton Primary School, Strathaven

Fair Trade

Some folk like to buy and sell
And make a profit from it
They never think of other folk
Who's lives just can't afford it.

They like to keep them poor and down
Oppressed and in the gutter
And seem to take a great offence
If they *'fair trade'* should mutter.

Fair trade is all these poor folk want
A chance to make the grade
A chance to live a better life
Not huge wealth to parade.

Peter Hastings (11)
Gilmourton Primary School, Strathaven

My Sister

She talks alot
Like a parrot
She always forgets things
Like my presents.
She has different coloured hair
Every week.
She's always kind,
Even when she's mad.
She always wears fake tan
And makes herself look brown
She works in Gap
All day long.

Erin Hastings (9)
Gilmourton Primary School, Strathaven

The Cook!

There once was a cook
But he couldn't find his book
He started to chop
But he stopped at the shop
So he looked for some prawns
But everyone yawns.
He went to the library
But met a canary
So the cook went home
And said 'Hi' to his gnome.
So he quit his job
And called himself Bob
And leapt into bed
And banged his head
And fell fast asleep,
And that was the last of the cook Bob.

Victoria Lennox (9)
Gilmourton Primary School, Strathaven

The Crazy Picture

I came across a crazy picture,
The craziest there was!
Once I'd thought about it,
It looked like the Wizard of Oz!
As many blues as you can imagine
Spread all over the page!
If it starts to bite, put it in a cage!
A big door open wide
Probably a place you can hide!
Passageway straight as can be
Plus it is very wee!

Jaimie Crozer (10)
Gilmourton Primary School, Strathaven

Witches Are Wicked

Witches are wicked
They turn you into toads and frogs
They are so wicked
They have warts of their face
And spots on their legs and arms
They have big brooms to fly on
And they scream wicked!
It is horrible, it's like *argh!*
Wicked.

Mitchell Saunders (8)
Glenluce Primary School, Newton Stewart

The Living Room Carpet

One day I was sitting in the sitting room
Doing my knitting in that room
Suddenly a flash of light
And I was whizzing through the sky
I saw loads of things
Even a lady with her apple pie!

Caitlin Davis (7)
Glenluce Primary School, Newton Stewart

My Pet Cat

My pet is a cat
She likes to eat rats
When she sits on the mat
She sleeps right away
When she wakes up
She ran out of the house
And down the street
And never came back.

Jenni Hastie (9)
Glenluce Primary School, Newton Stewart

Pets

Some pets run about
Some just sit and stare
But others curl up and sit
In front of the fire.

You might like a hamster
Who runs in a wheel
Maybe a dog
To jump about and bark
But best of all a little cat
To curl up on your lap.

Caty Cameron (8)
Glenluce Primary School, Newton Stewart

Friday Morning

On Friday morning I'm happy, happy, happy
At school I am yappy, yappy, yappy
I eat and drink
And think, think, think
I always worry, worry, worry
And always am in a hurry, hurry, hurry.

Lorna Rae (9)
Glenluce Primary School, Newton Stewart

Nature

Oh I love nature it's simply clear
With all the birds and bees.
I love when the butterflies flutter by
And the caterpillars wriggle away.
Oh how I love nature
Oh how I love nature
Oh how I love nature
It's simply clear!

Emma Miskimmins (9)
Glenluce Primary School, Newton Stewart

Cats

Cats, cats, they chase mice
Cats, cats they like mice
All through the night
Cats eyes glow in the dark
They lurk in corners
And scare the mice from the holes
And alleyways that give passageways to mice.

Hannah McIntosh (9)
Glenluce Primary School, Newton Stewart

Slippers

The thing with slippers
Is that they always fall off
The best thing to do with them
Is put them in the loft
And if you buy a new pair
It's best to have a back standing there
Now lets go back to the slippers in the loft
Now the front is falling off
And now all that's left are the soles.

Caroline McQuistin (8)
Glenluce Primary School, Newton Stewart

My Family

My mum said 'I've been thinking'
I thought she said 'I am shrinking'
My dad phoned last night
After that I turned off the light
When I woke up it was bright
I read a chapter of my book
Then I went to see my cousin Luke.

Morgan McIlwrick (9)
Glenluce Primary School, Newton Stewart

My Crazy Cat

My pet is a cat
It likes to eat a rat
Mostly it makes a mess of its mat
My cat lives in a flat
It always eats biscuits
It's getting puffy
Some people call him scruffy
He's my cat
He lives in a flat
He is a crazy cat
My crazy cat made me buy his flat
I bought some cookies
He just ate all of them
I said you're not the boss of me!
And I chased him out of the flat
I hate my cat!

Rorie White (8)
Glenluce Primary School, Newton Stewart

The Writer Of This Poem

(Based on 'The Writer of this Poem' by Roger McGough)

The writer of this poem . . .
Is as sensitive as glass
Soft like silk
So much class.

Mysterious like a cat
Friendly like a dog
As smart as an owl
Strong as a log.

Bright like the sun
Sweet like honey
Nice like flowers
Cute as a bunny.

Eve Spears (11)
Glenluce Primary School, Newton Stewart

The Spring

The spring
Calls out to buds
Which burst from bare branches
Trees are showing hints of green
New life.

Summer
Mixed with the sun
The trees look good fun
Mixed with the different colours.

Autumn
Autumn is cool
Animals are still young
Lots and lots of leaves on the ground
Brown leaves.

Winter
Winter is white
Lots of children playing
Lots of adults moving out
Loud shivers.

Shona Rennie (11)
Glenluce Primary School, Newton Stewart

The Penguin

I am stubby and white and black
I have an arched back
I waddle and I slide
Through the snow and ice
We sit and huddle but we don't cuddle
And I wait for a tap tap tapping
I am small and I know I will never be tall.

Elizabeth Crawfurd (8)
Glenluce Primary School, Newton Stewart

Woodland - Cinquain

The spring
Calls out to buds
Which burst from bare branches
Trees are showing a hint of green
New life

Summer
Brings out flowers
Yellow, red, pink and blue
So that is summer just for you
And me.

Autumn
Leaves are falling
Forming a crisp carpet
Bringing a lovely new fresh smell
Autumn.

Winter
It's cold outside
As dark nights draw closer
Animals are hibernating
Winter.

Kirstie McHarrie (12)
Glenluce Primary School, Newton Stewart

The Panther

As the panther creeps upon its prey
The rabbit, it hears no sound
The panther circles it round and round
Then with one big bound
It leaps on it like it was a tiny bug.
Walking home, looking very smug,
It gives the rabbit to its cub.

Sophie Forster (9)
Glenluce Primary School, Newton Stewart

Footie

When I score
I shout for more
Hitting the post
When I cannot boast.

I hate missing
but I'm great at dribbling
If I score a goal
I look like Andy Cole.

I'm good at free kicks though
I like the whistle to say go,
Half the time I hit the bar,
In golf I'd likely get a par.

When it comes to a foul
There always will be a growl
I'll end up with the free kick
Usually for taking the mick.

At the end of the day
The players get their pay
For playing the game
That has no shame!

Ewan Cameron (11)
Glenluce Primary School, Newton Stewart

My Dog

My dig
Is called Josh
And it's always looking very posh
It's a wee Scottish terrier
And it came form Siberia.

My dog
It's as cute as cute can be
Just like me!

Kayley McKie (11)
Glenluce Primary School, Newton Stewart

Fallen

Grey fairy
Grey feathered wings lie damp at her shoulder
Her face drenched in tears
Her eyes filled with sorrow
Her mind filled with fears.

Pale pale skin is wrapped round her body
Nothing but skin and bone there
Her hands are cold and shaking
But she doesn't care.

There seems to be no hope for her
Her sisters bright and cheery
With their beauty and glee
Her not beautiful and weary.

But wait. Hope. She can get out of this hell
Make her come back from this evil
Only time will tell. Here it comes hope for her
But then it goes away like a snowflake on a river
On a river a second but then gone forever.

Grey feathered wings lie damp at her shoulders
Her face drenched in tears
Her eyes filled with sorrow mind filled with fears.
It's hard to believe that she was pretty
Hair bright like pollen
None of that matters now
A fairy no longer.
Fallen.

Lauren McQuistin (11)
Glenluce Primary School, Newton Stewart

The Sun

The sun is like a golden ball in the sky above
The sun is great in the sky and on my bedroom wall
When it's not in sight of us someone else can see it
The sun is just great.

Andrew King (10)
Glenluce Primary School, Newton Stewart

My Pets

My pet is a little pink pig
His mother isn't that big
He lives with my mice
Who are not very nice
And teased him by doing a jig.

My pet is a lovely big sheep
Who kept jumping into our jeep
She ate up my shoe
And my jacket up too
Now she has to work for her keep.

My pet is a smelly green frog
Who was nearly eaten up by my dog
He began to sing
My ears started to ring
And he ran away into the fog.

Laura Paterson (11)
Glenluce Primary School, Newton Stewart

Food!

Chips, curry, chicken too
Pizza, pasta what to choose?
Fish or beef, I don't care
Salad with cheese, that's fair.
Anything I can stuff inside
Anything toasted or anything fried
Chocolate cake or Chinese nice
I'm in one lovely paradise!

Ruth Smedley (12)
Glenluce Primary School, Newton Stewart

King Harry

Old King Harry
Had a son called Barry
Who hated to marry
The girl called Sally.

Said King Harry
To young Barry
'You must marry
That girl called Sally.'

Said young Barry
To King Harry
'I will not marry
That girl called Sally.'

But in the end
Old King Harry
Made young Barry
Marry young Sally.

Chelsea Aitken (11)
Glenluce Primary School, Newton Stewart

Spanish Limerick

There once was a young girl from Spain
Who always had back pain
She woke in the night
To a terrible fright
And found she was out in the rain.

Callum Miskimmins (11)
Glenluce Primary School, Newton Stewart

Vikings

Once upon a rhyme
back in Viking times
those bearded men with such hairy faces
invaded all the local places.
They killed all the people with an axe
and a sword
but after a while they got bored.
The Vikings were all alone
so they decided to sail back home!

They climbed on their humungous boat
And they sailed away, they were finally afloat
But then the clouds began to loom
So they now knew they'd met their doom.
Up from the sea came a giant creature
With a rather scary feature
It had a giant set of teeth
Which caused the Vikings lots of grief.

Henry Crawfurd (11)
Glenluce Primary School, Newton Stewart

Sports

S wimming and soccer
P ole vault and polo
O lympics and other sports
R ugby and rounders
T ennis
S hooting too.

Kay Wilson (11)
Glenluce Primary School, Newton Stewart

Think Positive

T ell your mum, a teacher or a friend,
H opes and thoughts, your life will never end
I n your mind it will always stay
N ot like you can wish it away
K eep calm, they're really not worth it!

P hysical and mental, they think it's cool,
O nly the bully looks like the fool.
S tand up for yourself, you know you can,
I t's not as hard as pushing a van.
T he bully is the coward, it is not you,
I enjoy life, make sure you do too!
V ery unhappy, bullies make me,
E njoy your life, you'll soon see!

Hannah Mathieson & Fiona Caldwell (10)
Inchinnan Primary School, Inchinnan

Tell Someone

T alk to someone to help you
E ven if it is a close friend
L ook for a teacher
L et someone know you are being bullied

S ad bullies, they don't know what they are doing
O nly bullies are the stupid ones
M ad people hitting and shouting
E ventually they will leave you alone
O ffending you in every possible way
N agging you, bragging you, hurting your feelings
E njoy the rest of your life like you should.

Arran Dulai (11)
Inchinnan Primary School, Inchinnan

Abusive Bullying

A buse is when people are hit and shouted at
B ullies are cowards and they don't like flowers
U se your sense and tell a friend
S tick up for yourself and remember your friends are there for you
E ach day keeps fading away because bullies are there to annoy
you.

Dylan Connor & Darran Sims (10)
Inchinnan Primary School, Inchinnan

Bullies

B ig bullies
U nder control fools
L ike stealing money
L ike not eating honey
I t may be wrong
E ither sing a song
S top the *bullies!*

Fraser Reid (10) & Stephen McColl (11)
Inchinnan Primary School, Inchinnan

Friends

F riends are good
R eady to help
I n case you're being bullied
E nd of the road
N ever again
D etention shall never end for them
S tory shall now end.

Ryan Adam (10)
Inchinnan Primary School, Inchinnan

Racism

R acism is bad
A scend the people who are sad
C ritical bullying
I t is sad and it is pulling
S ome of your courage down
M ust tell a teacher and don't frown.

Christopher Keown (11)
Inchinnan Primary School, Inchinnan

Bullying

B ig bad bullies are the worst!
U gly and annoying
L ittle or big bullies are always *cowards!*
L only kids are picked on
Y ou don't know why bullies are mean
I t's never your fault if this happens
N ever listen to them as they call you names
G *o and tell someone!*

Stewart Fox & Courtney McClure (10)
Inchinnan Primary School, Inchinnan

Mental

M ean and annoying
E ach day gets worse
N asty and no friends
T ears is what they like
A nd there are nasty people
L onely they are.

Callum Blair & Stewart Brown (10)
Inchinnan Primary School, Inchinnan

Prejudice

P rimary should be fun, I guess so
R ough and rude, it hurts me so
E njoy school my mother says in the morning
J ust one hour till play time - *oh no!*
U ncomfortable and sore at night
D o I want to live like this? .
I don't know is it worth the risk?
C an I have the courage to ask for help?
E njoy it! Mother I can't! I'm being bullied!

Kayleigh Nardini & Gemma Westwood (10)
Inchinnan Primary School, Inchinnan

Bullying

B ullying is heartbreaking
U psetting and tearful
L ife is a misery with a tyrant about
L onely and gloomy, nothing to live for
Y elled and shouted at, abusing and harmful
I gnored and left out
N ot worth living
G iant bullies are wicked, spoiled and rotten.

Nicola Sheerin & Danuta McPherson (10)
Inchinnan Primary School, Inchinnan

Friend!

F riends forever bullies in the river
R ight we are, but they won't go far
I diots! Don't care they always swear
E ach day keeps fading away
N o bullies are sad, they are always glad
D umb they are, we will go far.

David Mimnagh (10) & Lewis Kerr (11)
Inchinnan Primary School, Inchinnan

Bullying

B e aware of bullying
U se options like telling the teacher
L earn not to worry
L osers! That's what bullies are
Y our friends will help you if you tell them
I think bullying is stupid
N o one should make you feel down
G reat friends will stick by you no matter what.

Callum McGregor (10) & Daniel Wilson (11)
Inchinnan Primary School, Inchinnan

Bullies

B ullies are cowards
U ntidy and angry in class
L ose their temper easily
L ike only other bullies
I mportant only to themselves
E nvy people's happy lives
S ome bullies just want a happy life

Greg McBride, Kyle McCrae & Johnny Morrison (10)
Inchinnan Primary School, Inchinnan

Pets

Rabbits hopping from place to place
Dogs barking while they chase.

Cats hunting in the night
Mice getting such a fright.

Fish are swimming in the cool
They are happy in the pool.

Stick insects are on the bark
Shredding their skin to look like a branch.

Georgia Todd (9)
Kilchrenan Primary School, Taynuilt

My Favourite Things

I like eating chicken curry
I like my pink blanket
Because it is furry.
Playing with my friends I also like,
And playing on my mountain bike.

I like wearing my nice blue jeans
I like having funny dreams
I like playing in the park
I really like it
When it's dark.

I like sitting in the sun
It is really so much fun
I like going out to eat
Somewhere fancy,
Anywhere is a treat.

Those are some of my favourite things
Eating and playing and other things.

Jade Sutherland (11)
Kilchrenan Primary School, Taynuilt

Tiger

Orange and black stalker
Padded paw walker
Antelope killer
Yellow eyes
Swatting flies
Lurking in grass
Ready to pounce
Lying in the sun
A big roar.

Euan Meldrum (9)
Kilchrenan Primary School, Taynuilt

Snow Is . . .

Snow is a curious thing
People say there is a blanket of snow
But if you were under it, you would die.

Snow is a sad thing
When it has gone all sleety
It disappears.

Snow is a beautiful thing
But there is nothing less beautiful
when it has been walked over.

Snow is a cruel thing
It stops the deer from eating
And it kills the tiny birds.

Snow is a wonderful thing
It covers the mountains with
icing sugar.

Snow is a happy thing
When children are playing
and making snowmen.

Snow is my favourite thing.

Chloe Wilkie (11)
Kilchrenan Primary School, Taynuilt

Dogs

Bone licker
Cat chaser
Stick catcher
An old dog in the summer sun
Is much too lazy to run
He rolls on the ground
Until he is found
And then it's time for tea.

Benjamin Bartholomew (8)
Kilchrenan Primary School, Taynuilt

The Seasons

Winter is when the snow falls
People like to make snowmen
Throwing snowballs at their friends.
Spring is when lambs are born
Lambs are running to their mothers
When older they turn into sheep.
Summer is when all the flowers come up
The bees are coming to the trees
They eat pears and plums.
In summer you can catch fish in a dish.
Autumn is when we roll in the leaves
They look all bare
But don't worry there will be a new layer in spring.

Joy Palmer (8)
Kilchrenan Primary School, Taynuilt

Trees

In the winter trees go white
They sway in the shadows of the night.
I watch the shadows of the trees
And the busy buzzing bees.
In the day the birds sit and rest
Some are busy building their nest.
In the wind the trees do sway
Often in the middle of the day.
I watch the trees grow and grow
Until foresters come and cut them low.

Jodi Sutherland (8)
Kilchrenan Primary School, Taynuilt

Birds

Swallows gliding through the air
Landing on the trees so tall
Snuggling down in their warm beds
Laying chicks all fluffy and small
Owls hooting in the night
Giving people quite a fright
Swooping down in their gentle flight
Magpies flying in the window
Stealing a spoon from my hand
Taking it to their nest so grand
Let it glisten in the sun
Look at them they're having great fun!

Sarah Wilkie (8)
Kilchrenan Primary School, Taynuilt

Weather

Rain go away
We want the sun to stay
There are no twisters here
But that thunder's getting near
Powerful is lightning
Wind and darkness is frightening
If there's a gale
The TV signal might fail
The sleet is bold
The snow is cold
Weather changes all the time.

Calum Galbraith (10)
Kilchrenan Primary School, Taynuilt

Strange

Dull sky and yellow sun
Dark night and bright light
Happy person and bad feelings
Nice water and bad taste
Smooth rock and rough ground
Lovely school and bad teachers
Bad poem and good words
Good country and bad weather
Big letters and small words
Large person and tiny germ
Small world and huge space
Strange feeling and brilliant emotion
Sharp knife and blunt blade
Good colour and bad hair
Lots of countries and one world.

Aron Wright (10)
Kilchrenan Primary School, Taynuilt

A Dream

In a dream you can turn into a mermaid
And dive into the deep blue sea.
In a dream you can turn into my friend
And say hello to me.
In a dream you can build a rocket
And fly up to the moon.
In a dream you can be a king
And eat from a silver spoon.
In a dream you can float on a cloud
Or be a person in a giant crowd.

Joshua Bartholomew (8)
Kilchrenan Primary School, Taynuilt

City

Cars bustling
Traffic lights
Car indicators flashing

People walking
People cycling
People all around

Cars speeding, police chasing
Cars crashing, ambulances coming
Fires starting, fire brigade putting them out

Dogs barking
Cats sneaking
Pigeon squawking in the sky.

Bin men collecting waste
Guide dogs helping the blind
Teachers helping us to learn to read and write.

Niall Sinclair (11)
Kilchrenan Primary School, Taynuilt

Favourite Things

Ice cream milkshakes
Best is vanilla.
Bacon, sausages
Fried and tender.
Dogs, cats, pups, kittens,
Soft and cuddly,
Fast and fun.
Maths, spelling
Best is maths.
These are some of my favourite things.

Callum Leitch (10)
Kilchrenan Primary School, Taynuilt

Football

F ootball, football in the net I scored a goal and they got beat
O ur team's the best in the world
O ne-nil was the score
T he best that's us
B eautiful blue tops and white shorts
A ball in the sky, wow! It's high
L ove from the fans. It's good to play
L aughing at the other team - let's play again.

Adam Blades (8)
Kirkshaws Primary School, Coatbridge

My Cat

My cat plays all the time
She never sleeps
She runs around mad
She drives me bonkers
She runs that much she's unstoppable
My cat plays all the time.

Mark Cappie (8)
Kirkshaws Primary School, Coatbridge

My Puppy

My puppy is cute and clever
My puppy is funny and bright
When I come home my puppy is happy and bright
When it goes out to play it sprints all around
My puppy is funny and bright
My puppy is cute and clever.

Amanda McFarlane (8)
Kirkshaws Primary School, Coatbridge

My Puppy

My puppy, my puppy
Eats any kind of fish even a guppy.
She's cute, she's funny,
She was a lot of money.
I love her, she's sweet,
She likes my feet.
She's full of beans.
I don't know what she means.
When she's scared her ears go up.
You can never shut her up.
My puppy, my puppy,
I should call her Lucky.
She's the best.
She's better than all the rest!

Melissa Moran (9)
Kirkshaws Primary School, Coatbridge

Football

Football, football, I like football
It is my favourite sport and I win all the time.
I won 2-1 and it was cool
Then I scored all the goals
Football, football, I like football.

Connor Bruin (8)
Kirkshaws Primary School, Coatbridge

My Puppy

My puppy is cute and fluffy
It likes to play with a ball
But it does not bite in a flash
So it just grabs you when it wants to.
My puppy is cute and fluffy.

Sean Gallacher (8)
Kirkshaws Primary School, Coatbridge

Football

F ootball, football it is cool
O nly I am the best
O ur team is the best
T en minutes to go and we were winning
B all went into the net then it was 2-0
A ll the fans were so happy that it was a goal
L ast minute - the whistle blew and we won it
L ovely! We won the cup.

Conlon Campbell (8)
Kirkshaws Primary School, Coatbridge

My Cat

Cat, cat go and scratch my back
Help me get the towel or I will fall out of the bath
Cat, cat why do you wear that hat all the time?
Going to chase the birds
I love cat, cat too.

Amy Brannen (8)
Kirkshaws Primary School, Coatbridge

Sword Fight

S unny day in Verona
W ith swords clashing!
O ne day
R omeo fell in love with the
D elightful Juliet.

F ighting, oh fighting Romeo and Juliet do not like their
   families fighting
I Romeo am fighting in the street
G etting married to the gorgeous Juliet
H appiness comes to the old people at
T he end.

Hannah Penman (9)
Musselburgh Burgh Primary School, Musselburgh

Years

First day, winter day
Cold winds are blowing, showers of rain are pouring.
The night before we stayed up 'til 12 o'clock
The clock going tick and tock
That night was warmed with celebration
Hot chocolate, parties, TV programme specials
After that we get to sleep, ready for tomorrow.

The days went by then spring you arrive!
Sun, small showers and daffodil fields.

The days go past and summer at last!
Endless sunshine the temperatures are high and barbecues every
night
You never want to go inside unless you want some ice cold water!
Warm starry nights that don't seem to last . . .

So then the season autumn comes, we shall need our coats again
Trees and leaves go together but because of the weather
they are separated
Bonfire night and Hallowe'en are the reasons why I love autumn!

Winter will come with rain, ice and snow
But Christmas is coming hip hip hooray!
Presents, mince pies, turkey dinner, and celebration
Then we start again!

First day, winter day, cold winds are blowing
Showers of rain are pouring.

Craig Milne (10)
Musselburgh Burgh Primary School, Musselburgh

Love Haiku

Romeo loves her
Kissing in the night's moonlight
Love is all around.

Katie McDonald (10)
Musselburgh Burgh Primary School, Musselburgh

Romeo And Juliet

'R omeo, Romeo my lovely star
   You make me so happy
O n the day you marry me
   I'll love you even more
M ontague hates the Capulets but we don't,
   We love each other
E nd the sword fights
   I don't want you hurt
O h Romeo I love you.'

   And

'J uliet, Juliet my little star
U nder the moon I know you love me
L ots and lots I love you
 I think you smell like a flower
E yes that twinkle like stars
T ell me you love me too.'

Claire Brenchley (9)
Musselburgh Burgh Primary School, Musselburgh

The Sword Fight

Montague and Capulet always fighting in the street.
They both will never live at peace.
Romeo Montague and Juliet Capulet love each other very much.
Darkness strikes when hating starts.
Tybalt Capulet kills Mercutio with the strike of a sword
Then is struck down himself.
Romeo's sword swooped up to Tybalt's neck.
He fell to the ground clutching his head.
Romeo got sent away and was told to never come back.
Romeo gave Juliet love's last kiss
They waved goodbye
Romeo went away missing Juliet very much.

Laura Robertson (10)
Musselburgh Burgh Primary School, Musselburgh

The Love Of Romeo And Juliet

J uliet and Romeo
U nderground in their tomb
L oving each other always
I n their town is peace now
E very day the families Montague and Capulet remember
T he love of Romeo and Juliet.

F or they met at the ball
O f Capulet and Romeo, a Montague,
R omeo was in trouble for now Tybalt knows.

R omeo was banished from the town
O ver back in town Juliet drank the potion
'M y loved one is dead' cried Romeo
'E very day I will just cry, so I must die as well'
O n and on the love of Romeo and Juliet will go on.

Hannah Thomson (9)
Musselburgh Burgh Primary School, Musselburgh

Happy

Happy is orange
Happy tastes like food
Happy smells like fish
Happy looks like a smile
Happy sounds like singing.

Corey Watt (10)
Musselburgh Burgh Primary School, Musselburgh

Fight Of Terror Haiku

Fighting in the street
Clashing banging noises fight
Fighting at the ball.

Ailsa Fraser (10)
Musselburgh Burgh Primary School, Musselburgh

The Fight

At one end of the cobbled square is a Capulet,
A Montague is at the alternate,
They circle each other,
Waiting, waiting for the moment to strike,
A crowd gathers squabbling for the best place,
Each fighter draws his sword,
The crowd falls silent,
Capulet dives in for the strike, swishing his fine weapon
but nothing meets it
The Montague is enraged,
He thrusts his dagger out blindly, hoping it will touch flesh,
Capulet moves in to meet the shining blade, blocking it with
his counter movement,
The next thing the spectators regard is a gory scene not for the
faint-hearted,
Another man is lying dead, Tybalt,
The Capulet's breath has been cut and the only man who stands
is the Montague,
Romeo Montague,
Knowing that the Prince would have him slain he runs for his life
and his one true love
Juliet Capulet.

Elspeth Wilson (9)
Musselburgh Burgh Primary School, Musselburgh

Romeo And Juliet Haiku

Tybalt kills one friend
Of Romeo Montague
Strikes revenge again.

Callum Hancock (10)
Musselburgh Burgh Primary School, Musselburgh

Romeo And Juliet

Romeo Montague and Juliet Capulet
The Montagues hate the Capulets
The Capulets hate the Montagues
They fight then light dies
The prince comes 'Banished from this town!'
He cried at Romeo.
A plan is invented by Friar Lawrence
A potion will make you look dead.
The nurse finds out that Juliet is dead,
The plan has worked or so she thought!
Romeo hears the tragic news but not the plan!
'I shall see her body at the temple'
'No!' He gets a different potion
That kills.
Goodbye my dear wife I will give you a kiss
And join you in Heaven.
Just then weak Juliet wakes up
'Oh Romeo why are you here?'
Death comes upon her!
'I will join you in Heaven young Romeo, my love is for you.
Oh sweet little dagger something so small.'
She pushes the dagger into her broken heart.

Natasha Young (10)
Musselburgh Burgh Primary School, Musselburgh

Love

L ove is in the air
O nly for one day
V erona's deadly cries
E cho love all around.

Robert MacFarlane (9)
Musselburgh Burgh Primary School, Musselburgh

Romeo Loves Juliet

R omeo loves Juliet
O n the
M ontague side
E verybody is fighting against the Capulets
O n Verona street.

L oving each other
O nly Romeo and Juliet
V erona's street they fight on
E ven Romeo
S tabs Tybalt.

J uliet loves Romeo
U ntil they die
L aid down
 I n a grave peacefully
E veryone listens to
T he story of Romeo and Juliet.

Samantha Bradley (10)
Musselburgh Burgh Primary School, Musselburgh

Romeo And Juliet

R omeo loves Juliet,
O nly Juliet he loves,
M ercutio is Romeo's best friend,
E verybody is fighting on the street,
O n the balcony in the Capulet house they talk.

A lways meeting, Romeo and Juliet are,
N ight falls and they say goodbye,
D eath lies upon Mercutio and Tybalt.

J uliet meets Romeo at the Capulet ball,
U nluckily Romeo and Juliet die,
L ying down dead together not moving at all,
 I n Verona there is a statue of Romeo and Juliet
E verybody is now friends both Montague and Capulet,
T ell people the story of Romeo and Juliet and they'll love it!

Leigh Chapman (9)
Musselburgh Burgh Primary School, Musselburgh

Romeo And Juliet

Click clack go the swords of Montague
Click clack go the swords of Capulet
They fight and they fight if only it would stop
This tragic event is calling death
If only they would just be friends
Verona would be a lot happier place.
Juliet of Capulet and Romeo of Montague get married
What a bad idea getting married coming from rival families
If someone found out there would be trouble
I wonder what will happen next?

Nicola Henry (9)
Musselburgh Burgh Primary School, Musselburgh

Verona

Verona is thrilling thunder
It is dying deer and leaping lions
Verona is clumpy curry
It is a nefarious nettle
Verona is raging red
It is sweating sweatshirts.

Cameron Craig (9)
Musselburgh Burgh Primary School, Musselburgh

Romeo And Juliet

'Romeo, Romeo, my star, that gives me light
Throughout the dark night.'

'Juliet, Juliet, my one and only love
That keeps my heart beating
Throughout the dark night.

Rebecca Scoots (9)
Musselburgh Burgh Primary School, Musselburgh

Capulet Vs Montague

They meet in the streets
And start up a fight
Tybalt and Mercutio
Argue at first sight.
Romeo says 'Stop'
They don't understand,
He pulls them apart
But Mercutio gets stabbed.
Romeo's anger takes over his mind,
He's incredibly angry
That his best friend has died,
He pulls out his sword
And pushes it in,
Tybalt's young body has no life in him.

Katherine Bryer (10)
Musselburgh Burgh Primary School, Musselburgh

Rockets And Blue Lights

Strong waves beat against the rocks like
bullets onto the sand.
Rockets shoot up into the air like a whale
rising from the sea
And as they hit the sky they
make a bang as if the world
has just collapsed beneath our feet.
The smell of soggy seaweed aims straight
for my nose.
The taste of the sea runs right through me.
The salvagers reach the shore out of breath.
I hear coughing and screaming as people
come to the rescue.
Finally the storm calms down and everybody
is safe.
I can go home now, to my bed, it's been a long night.

Kiah Taylor (11)
Netherton Primary School, Wishaw

Rockets And Blue Lights

Looking out to the wide, stretching sea
I watch as rockets go whizzing and whirling
into the air.
Murky, eye-stinging smoke simmers and
puffs out over the sky.
Distressful cries echo from the punctured
tanker.
Rockets sizzle, then explode into flight.
I can smell the salty water mixed with puffy,
grey smoke rising endlessly to the heavens
above, like metal to magnet.
I can taste embers from the smoke as it
approaches me.
I back away from the wreck, the ship, the
smoke and the fizzing rockets, into my house,
shelter under my bed cover and hope it's all
gone by morn.

Adam Port (10)
Netherton Primary School, Wishaw

The Butterfly

It flies so, so high
Up in the sky
Colours - red - blue - pink

The wings flutter
You can't hear it
Flying past you

I wonder what it eats
I wonder where it stays
I wonder will you stay in my garden.

Kimberley Wilson (7)
Raploch Primary School, Stirling

My Pigeon

I like holding Corky
I hold him carefully
He is the best flier
He wins trophies
I stroke his back
And the top of his head
I whisper 'Good luck'
He flies away
But always he comes back.

James Stewart (7)
Raploch Primary School, Stirling

At The Beach

Happy people at the beach
Playing with their dogs
Happy people making sandcastles
Playing beach volleyball
Happy people swimming in the sea
Playing splashing games with their friends
Happy people sunbathing and thinking
What a wonderful holiday.

Shannon Lafferty (8)
Raploch Primary School, Stirling

Where Else?

Where else can you jump in the waves
Where else can you paddle in the sea
Where else can you throw your beach ball for miles
Where else can you build a giant sandcastle
Where else can you have fun at the fair?
             Blackpool!

Sam Goodwillie (8)
Raploch Primary School, Stirling

Watching

The polar bear swimming in the water
Trying to catch a fish
Furry white coat
Black deep eyes
He comes to see me wave.

Naomi McCallum (7)
Raploch Primary School, Stirling

At The Beach

Children drawing pictures in the sand
Children splashing in the sea
Children having picnics
Children playing with beachballs
Children having so much fun!

Brooke Cameron (8)
Raploch Primary School, Stirling

Africa

Africa, continent of contrasts
Where life began.
Great deserts like colossal oceans of golden sand
Cover the land.
Deep green blankets of trees
Overlap these warm silky seas.
Sapphire blue snakes of water
Squirm across the arid land
And flowering cacti stand prickling below
Towering, snow peaked mountains.
Like overgrown chocolate cakes
Topped with sparkling white icing.
Making Africa, a place
I want to go.

Andrew Cox (11)
Ravenscraig Primary School, Greenock

Land Of Mystery

Africa - cradle of life
Egypt, with its vast waves of golden sand
Never again will the pharaohs rule
But their history will.

The Savannah
Where many creatures roam
Hungrily hunting, silently hiding
Even there, the mystery remains.

Tropical jungles, weird creatures
Venomous snakes, chameleons
How do they change colours?
That is a mystery.

Many people wonder
Many seek
But no one will discover the secret
Of the land of mystery.

Jamie Campbell (12)
Ravenscraig Primary School, Greenock

The Dark Continent

The dark continent of sandy dunes
Ballet dances of whirlwind storms
Cobalt lakes of glittering hands that wave
Calling you . . .

Africa, the cradle of life
Great lakes of precious water
Ancient cities of mud and clay
Now cities of skyscrapers, bungalows . . .

This land of mystery
Golden deserts, snow-capped peaks
That lure . . .

Jordan Gostelow (11)
Ravenscraig Primary School, Greenock

Africa

Africa - cradle of life, land of mysteries
Vast, scorching oceans of arid sand
Misty verdant carpets of wild jungle

Rivers like immeasurable, slithering serpents
Glistening in the dusk, snow-peaked mountains
Reach for the sky

Great pyramids echo of ancient Egyptians
Cunning and strong
Oasis, azure blue, refresh and cool

Palm trees and cactus - reservoirs of the Sahara
The cheetah and elephant, wonderful creatures
With people walk many miles for precious water

Africa - cradle of life, land of mysteries
An amazing place!

Karin Alexander (12)
Ravenscraig Primary School, Greenock

Cradle Of Life

The tip of the mountain is
Snowy white like an arctic polar bear
Contrast this with the dark green jungles
Of tropical plants
Giant, winding rivers flow
And slither like wild snakes
Through this vast continent
Strange birds fly across the lovely sunny sky
As colossal planes soar above them
The sun scorches the sandy deserts
As nomads ride across the hot, hot landscape
While the camels thirst for more and more water
And Africa goes into shadow in the crimson dusk.

David Nicholson (11)
Ravenscraig Primary School, Greenock

Continent Of Contrasts

Africa, the dark continent
As I look over the land
The cradle of all human life opens up to me
In the dense, verdant jungles
Trees wave, snakes slither
White, snowy, cold mountains
Glisten in the dusk
Vast oceans of golden sands soften
As people walk in the sunrise
While rivers twist and snake
Like a cold, blue night

Lions, lurk in the patchy ground as
Crocodiles and hippos
Wait in the clear waters to feed
Camels with heavy loads
Walk across the scorching Sahara
And buildings of steel and concrete
Stand watching in the cities
As snow peaked mountains stand
Still as statues in a museum
Who will ever see the beauty of this land?
It is a secret no one will discover.

Nicola Leith (11)
Ravenscraig Primary School, Greenock

My Dog

My dog is called Oscar,
She is lazy
Her nickname is 'Daisy'
She snores when she sleeps
And she barks when she needs something to eat.

She's got eyes like hazelnuts
And a nose like a normal mutt
She tries to be funny
And looks like a bunny,
And always chases cats
But never wears a hat.

She's a friendly dog
But hates my pet frog
She also likes meat,
And eats like the other dogs on the street.
I don't know why, but she likes pie,
The blueberry kind,
She's out of her mind,
But she's really one of a kind.

Ryan Clarke (10)
Rochsolloch Primary School, Airdrie

The Weather

I hate it when it rains
And it fills up all the drains
It gushes down my street
And wets all my feet

I hate it when it pours
And I have to play indoors
My mum says let's bake
So I make a yummy cake

On a lovely sunny day
I like to go out to play
My friends play with me
And sometimes stay for tea

I like to go to the park
And come home when it's dark
Then I go to bed
And wonder what's ahead.

Zoe Shanks (10)
Rochsolloch Primary School, Airdrie

My Cat Tinker

Tinker is my old black and white cat
He is handsome, brave but not too fat

I love him more than words can tell
He's the one thing I would never sell

He likes to go out and roam all day
But I know he's never far away

He knows what time I come home from school
He'll always be my black and white jewel

Although he's old and has a bad heart
He'll always be my little sweetheart.

Nicole Middleton (10)
Rochsolloch Primary School, Airdrie

Boys Best Friend

Boys need something in their life
Like toys, computers and sport,
But best of all! No not a wife!
A dog, to be your escort.

My dog is golden like the sun,
Wet nose, smooth coat and long tongue too,
He makes me happy, he's full of fun,
He's my best pal, Blue.

Each morning, after breakfast,
My duties, they are clear
Walkies, food and drinks at last
My doggy doesn't ask for much, but he's very dear.

My dog brings me lots of joy
He loves and protects me too.
I'm not angry when he steals my toy,
Because it's just my Blue.

Ian MacPherson (10)
Rochsolloch Primary School, Airdrie

My Year

January is frosty white and cold,
February is a month that is quick and bold,
March is the month that brings Easter near,
April is the month when Easter is here.
May is a time to swish a broom,
June is when all the flowers come to bloom.
July brings us fun and holiday cheer,
August starts school which some of us fear.
September has a weekend where we all chill out,
October has a week that school is out.
November is a cool month with thirty days in it,
December is full of Christmas spirit.

Heather Shea (11)
Rochsolloch Primary School, Airdrie

I Wonder Why

I wonder why I wonder
Why I come here every day
I wonder why I wonder
Why I just don't get to play.

Sometimes I wonder why
Sometimes I can tell
People who are naughty and
People who are swell.

I wonder why I wonder
Why people look me in the eye,
I wonder why I wonder
Why they keep me at short range
Maybe it's because my brother's face is
Rather strange.

I wonder why I wonder
Why I just can't tell a lie,
I wonder why I wonder
Why I wonder about soaring high
Where my soul may never die.

Josh Wallace (10)
Rochsolloch Primary School, Airdrie

Mice

I think mice are
Are really nice
Their eyes are
Beaded
Their tails are long they
Haven't got any brains at all.

Their claws
Are sharp
Their ears
Are pink
They scurry round the
House at night.

Their teeth nibble
Things they shouldn't touch
Their noses
Are pink
Their whiskers twitch
They can smell cheese
A mile away.

I don't know anyone who likes them much
But I think mice are rather nice.

Kerry Johnson (11)
Rochsolloch Primary School, Airdrie

My Grandad

My grandad's name is Billy,
He is often very silly,
When he is being silly,
We all say,
'You are a silly sausage Billy.'

He is a man full of brains
But he pretends it strains
He is very good at maths
But he prefers laughs.

He is married to my gran
Who is cleverer than any man.
She has curly, orange, red hair,
So you can tell when she is there.

His wife is called Christina,
But he says 'Christine'
One of his favourite sayings must be,
'Come on Christine where's my cup of tea?'

He is the father of my mother,
Also her two sisters and her brother,
My grandma is their mother,
And she is better than any other.

My grandad is so great
And he is never ever late,
He has a shiny red car,
So he can travel far.

My grandad is so kind,
So he doesn't really mind,
If me or my cousins are bad
He just says he's glad,
That we are not always that bad.

Ailsa McRae (10)
Rochsolloch Primary School, Airdrie

My Book

My book is a great book
It's called Peter Pan
Whose enemy is Captain Hook
He has two enemies Peter Pan and Croc
Croc one day swallowed a clock
Every time Croc comes near
You can always hear
'Tick-tock, tick-tock.'

There is also a girl called Wendy
Who thinks she's very trendy
She thinks the world of Peter Pan
And thinks that he's a great man.

Also a boy called John
Whose brain has always shone
He wears a top hat
And thinks of things in two seconds flat.

Then there is Michael
Who always takes his teddy Ted
To sleep beside him in bed
He is always behind
But he never declined.

Now, my favourite, The Lost Boys
Their weapons are just like toys
They always fight,
But never share,
Not even one pear.

At last Peter Pan
Who has a mini sword
And never wants to become a man,
In his hat he's got a feather
And is happy whatever the weather.

Darren Pryde (10)
Rochsolloch Primary School, Airdrie

My Gran

My gran is sweet because . . .
She gives me sweets
And lots of treats
She gives me money
And it is quite funny.
I cannot say
I cannot tell
But
Gran you are really swell.
Flowers are lovely
Like you Gran
Sweets are sweet
Like you Gran
I love you Gran
And that is why you're
My gran.

Ainsley Broadley (10)
Rochsolloch Primary School, Airdrie

Rubbish Is . . .

Rubbish is junk that is lying at the bottom of a smelly
horrible black dustbin.
It is boys and girls picking up cans, foil and tins
that people drop on the street and are too lazy to
put in the bin.
It is a paper bag that is flying in the breeze.
It is foil that is flying in people's faces
in the rustling wind.
It is broken glass in the recycling pit.
It is chewing gum stuck to your trainers
and stuck to the ground.
It is a man throwing a cigarette out the window.
Rubbish is a robin stuck in a juice bottle in the garden.

Emma Laird (9)
St Andrew's RC Primary School, Gorebridge

My Mum

You are the shining sun on a summer's day.
You are the blue waves crashing on the shore.
You are a friendly dolphin swimming in the sea.
You are the twinkling stars in the sky.
You are the cool raindrops hanging from a leaf.
You are the soft snow floating to the ground.
You are the fresh buds on a blossom tree.
You are a blood-red rose swaying in the wind.
You are the sweet smell of lavender growing in a valley.
You are the golden corn soaking up the sun.
You are a beautiful butterfly fluttering in the air.
You are the deathly-white moon, casting shadows on the trees.
You are a tiny robin fighting the winter air.
You are the whistling wind blowing through the sky.
You are the fresh green grass on an April's day.
You are my mum and I love you!

Kelly McLeary (10)
St Andrew's RC Primary School, Gorebridge

If I Was An Iron Giant

If I was an iron giant I would be so clean,
If I was an iron giant you would see me gleam,
If I was an iron giant you would see my face,
If I was an iron giant you wouldn't keep
Up with my pace,
If I was an iron giant I would live in
Perth,
If I was an iron giant I would rule the
Earth,
If I was an iron giant I would be called
Lee,
If I was an iron giant, but I can't be an
iron giant because I'm just me!

Alana Hennessey (9)
St Andrew's RC Primary School, Gorebridge

Don't

Don't kiss the dog or you will end up like a frog
Don't be cheeky to your mum or you will get a smack
on the bum.
Don't dig a hole or you will find a mole.
Don't be cheeky to your gran or you will end up in a van.
Don't drink out of a mug or you will turn into a slug.
Don't touch the pot because it is too hot.
Don't hit the groom with a broom.
Don't sit on that chair or pull out hairs.
Don't use the mop or you will pop.
Don't eat peas or you will get fleas.
Don't kick your shoe at the loo.
Don't be cheeky to your dad or he will get mad.
Don't throw that mat or rip that hat.
Don't eat sweets or play with your meat.

Samantha Laing (10)
St Andrew's RC Primary School, Gorebridge

Candle Burning

Candle burning as red as
a rose sprouting in the spring.
Candle burning blue like waves
swaying in the ocean.
Candle burning as yellow as the sun burning
in the sky.
Candle stretching like frogs legs as it jumps
off the ground.
Candle burning as spiky as the Eiffel Tower.
Candle burning as orange as an orang-utan
swinging high in the air.
Candle burning as peacefully as a
bird soaring in the sky.

Andrew Knott (9)
St Andrew's RC Primary School, Gorebridge

My Friend

He's a bright lamp in my dark room
He's a baboon eating fruit.
He's the smell of a cheery red rose in the bright
green grass.
He's the sound of a smiley face laughing.
He's the blazing-hot sun on the beach.
He's a pizza smiling in the hot cooker.
He's the colourful flowers in summer.
He's the colour of shining gold.

Anne Hume (9)
St Andrew's RC Primary School, Gorebridge

My Friend

He's a cooker sizzling very loudly.
He's a cheetah racing through the plains.
He's the smell of hot bubbling pizza on my plate.
He's the sound of high-pitched laughter in a silent room.
He's the middle of a mild afternoon.
He's a bright sunny day.
He's a plate of spaghetti wriggling on the floor.
He's the start of summer.
He's a yellow stripe speeding on the road.

Geordie Anderson (10)
St Andrew's RC Primary School, Gorebridge

Don't

Don't let the cat eat the rat.
Don't let the goat get the boat.
Don't cook your book.
Don't put glue in your shoe.
Don't pull hairs out of bears.

Eilidh Yule (10)
St Andrew's RC Primary School, Gorebridge

Rubbish Is . . .

Rubbish is junk sitting in your bin
removed to the valley pit in-between the hills.
It is a boy throwing cans out of a window.
It is mice going round and round stuck in a bottle.
It is a boy picking up litter.
it is traps for mice.
Rubbish is people picking up litter.

Benjamin Allison (8)
St Andrew's RC Primary School, Gorebridge

Rubbish Is . . .

Rubbish is rustling foil blowing down the street.
It is dogs having a dancing contest over a McMinis box.
It is a man throwing a paper bag and it being stuck in wire.
It is people putting pockets of candy wrappers in the sea.
It is men who are drunk and throwing glass bottles.
It is people feeding animals and picking up rubbish.
it is a girl taking a bottle to a bottle bank.

Euan Richards (8)
St Andrew's RC Primary School, Gorebridge

The Colour Of Me

When I am crying
I am as blue as the blue sea.

When I am friendless
I am as white as the cloudy sky.

When I am mad
I am as red as red paint on the school wall.

Andrew Blair (9)
St Andrew's RC Primary School, Gorebridge

Rubbish Is . .

Rubbish is part of our smelly bin
It is a girl chucking all her litter away
It is bursting black bags blowing in the wind
It is chewing gum stuck to your foot
It is a boy picking up all the rubbish he can find in the street.
It is junk in the street that birds are eating.
It is lots of bouncing bears ballet dancing around all the
smelly rubbish in Edinburgh Zoo.
It is one kind girl happy to pick up all the stinky rubbish.

Nikki Clifford (9)
St Andrew's RC Primary School, Gorebridge

Rubbish Is . . .

Rubbish is a tin can rolling down the street
It is the junk at the bottom of your bin.
it is foil floating in the wind.
It is a plastic bag stuck in a tall tree.
It is chewing gum on the bottom of your shoe.
It is paper rustling in the street.
It is glass bottles in the bottle bank.
Rubbish is a cat and dog fighting over a crisp packet.

Jaydene Hamilton (9)
St Andrew's RC Primary School, Gorebridge

Rubbish Is . . .

Rubbish is a girl taking bottles to the bottle bank.
It is some junk that rustles in the wind.
It is litter that people drop when there is no bin.
It is an apple core thrown out the window.
It is chewing gum stuck to your shoe.
Rubbish is a little boy picking up rubbish
And putting it in the bin.

Claire McInally (8)
St Andrew's RC Primary School, Gorebridge

Rubbish Is . . .

Rubbish is a girl picking up bright green bottles and putting
                            them in the recycling bin.
It is bright white mice dancing and eating round a dirty crisp packet.
It is a clump of smelly junk which is a couple of months. It will
                            change into compost.
It is rabbits and foxes moving out of their homes because of all the
                            rubbish that has blown into their habitat.
It is bugs getting legs broken off by getting stuck in sticky
                            chewing gum.
It is animals dying because of eating rubbish and becoming
                            very ill.
It is greasy oil running into ponds and killing pond animals.
It is litter being thrown onto the road from a car.
It is a glass bottle being thrown in the tip instead of being
                            reused or recycled which can save energy.

Shannon Allan (9)
St Andrew's RC Primary School, Gorebridge

Rubbish Is . . .

Rubbish is a boy recycling clothes.
It is messy junk blowing happily in a valley.
It is a boy's shoe stuck to chewing gum.
It is a glass jam jar smashed.
It is a road with crisps scattered along the ground.
It is a banana skin on the ground.
it is a Kit-Kat on the smooth path.
It is kids dropping sweet papers.
It is an apple core along a very long path.
It is a jug of empty milk jug in a valley.

Katey McGee (8)
St Andrew's RC Primary School, Gorebridge

Rubbish Is . . .

Rubbish is something that takes up too much energy.
It is something that we can reuse, reduce and recycle.
It is ducks dancing in polluted water.
It is a boy with chewing gum stuck to his shoe.
It is the thing that we don't need so much of.
It is a man picking up litter and putting it in a recycling box.
It is smelly smoke from a plastic factory.
It is dust that we breathe in and it makes us choke.
It is horrible hankies lying on the ground.
It is annoying aluminium that cut my finger when I picked it up.
It is glass with a drop of blood from a sparrow.
Rubbish is banana skins lying on the ground.

Rosie Anderson (8)
St Andrew's RC Primary School, Gorebridge

Rubbish Is . . .

Rubbish is a plastic bag rustling in the breeze.
It is a man throwing a sandwich out of the car window.
It is a boy spitting disgustingly onto the solid ground.
It is a duck ducking for food in polluted water.
It is chewing gum on the sole of your trainer.
It is glass bottles in the grass which have a little shrew
trapped in them.
It is a beautiful swan stuck in a fishing rod line.

Emily Brown (9)
St Andrew's RC Primary School, Gorebridge

Rubbish Is . . .

Rubbish is junk thrown out the door and just left there.
It is a boy picking up rubbish that people left there.
It is a boy chucking a glass bottle onto the grass.
Rubbish is blowing about in thin air.

Robyn Faughnan (8)
St Andrew's RC Primary School, Gorebridge

Rubbish Is . . .

Rubbish is a girl taking bottles to the bottle bank.
It is litter that people drop when there are no bins.
It is glass bottles, cans and tins rolling about in the wind.
It is some junk that rustles in the wind.
it is some drunk people throwing away chip boxes.
It is an apple core that has been thrown on the ground.
It is some bubblegum stuck to a shrew's foot.
It is a boy picking up a pile of plastic bags to reuse.
It is a bird stuck in a tin with it tweeting to get out.
Rubbish is some chewing gum stuck to your shoe.

Becky McEwan (8)
St Andrew's RC Primary School, Gorebridge

Rubbish Is . . .

Rubbish is a tin can rolling around in the wind.
It is junk that is at the bottom of your bin.
It is food at the bottom of your smelly compost heap.
It is a glass bottle smashed by a drunk person.
It is a piece of tinfoil being blown away.
It is a plastic bottle being kicked by a boy
who wants to become a football player.
It is a paper being blown away.
Rubbish is clothes that don't fit you being chucked out.

Stuart Reid (9)
St Andrew's RC Primary School, Gorebridge

Rubbish Is . . .

Rubbish is tins and cans and smelly pans whacking apples away.
It is foil flying into people's faces like a hurricane.
It is banana skins sticking to the road.
It is a cake flying out of a car window.
It is a bag burning and destroying wildlife.
Rubbish is a mouse stuck in a bottle.

Daniel McConnell (8)
St Andrew's RC Primary School, Gorebridge

Rubbish Is . . .

Rubbish is cans that rattle and rattle, in the wind.
It is people who throw rubbish and all the rats come.
It is crisp packets that blow away when you throw them away.
It is new calendars that have just been bought and thrown away.
It is an apple core that has been thrown away and lots of
ants come and crawl about the apple core.
It is rustling tinfoil that blows about in the wind.
It is girls that throw sweet wrappers away.
It is two dogs that bark as loud and burst your eardrums
Just over a bone!
It is newspapers that have been thrown into the recycling bins.
It is boys and girls who throw chip bags on the ground.
It is people who throw rubbish and all the rats come.
It is when people throw away chewing gum and you will
get it stuck to your foot.
Rubbish is when you put rubbish in the wrong place.

Sara Henderson (9)
St Andrew's RC Primary School, Gorebridge

Rubbish Is . . .

Rubbish is a boy picking up smelly rubbish and
putting it into the bin.
It is a paper flying in the wind across the sky and
into the dirty sea.
It is recyclable leaves flying across the street in the breeze.
It is a plastic bag getting burned and spreading
chemicals across the city.
It is a greasy chip bag on the pavement.
It is a mouse stuck in a glass bottle.
It is a boy putting glass bottles into a bottle bank.
Rubbish is a crisp bag blowing in the wind.

Jack Fraser (8)
St Andrew's RC Primary School, Gorebridge

Out In The Snow

Out in the snow I . . .
slide and shiver,
smile and laugh,
fall and throw snowballs,
shiver and shake,
play and have fun,
get damp and cold,
moan and scream,
fall and tumble,
sneeze and shiver,
thump and slip,
duck and slip.

Jemma Henderson (9)
St Andrew's RC Primary School, Gorebridge

Rubbish Is . . .

Rubbish is some bugs crawling in a packet
of cheese and onion crisps.
It is a paper bag flying through the bright blue sky.
It is a little girl singing while picking up rubbish
outside her garden.
It is some leaves falling off the bright green tree.
It is a glass bottle rolling through the wind down a really
steep hill.
It is some shiny tin foil rustling through the airy breeze.
It is a strong wind chasing after the rubbish.
It is rubbish that's not been thrown away but instead
turned into compost.

Louise Torrie (8)
St Andrew's RC Primary School, Gorebridge

I Am A . . .

I am a . . .
a tree burner
a room heater
a forest destroyer
a kettle boiler
a dinner cooker
a dung burner
a house destroyer
a food barbecuer
an animal frightener
a life destroyer
a people disfigurer
a coal burner
a cigarette lighter
an electricity maker
what am I?

Danielle Vass (10)
St Andrew's RC Primary School, Gorebridge

Candle Burning

Candle flickering angrily like a snake hissing.
Candle waving like a gazelle escaping from a predator.
Candle swaying like a palm tree in a hurricane.
Candle burning orange like tigers' fur.
Candle burning like lightning in the sky.
Candle burning blue like the Scottish saltire.
Candle peaceful like a sleeping baby.
Candle silent like a feather falling from the sky.
Candle pointy like a carving knife.
Candle ragged like a dog chewed rug.
Candle fat like a hippo.
Candle thin like sewing threads.

Matthew Allison (10)
St Andrew's RC Primary School, Gorebridge

I Am . . .

I am . . .
a circle maker
a window washer
a head clearer
a tree cleaner
a puddle fixer
a dog drencher
a hole filler
a flower feeder
a drop dripper
a splish splasher.
    What am I?

Ty Hennessey (9)
St Andrew's RC Primary School, Gorebridge

Rubbish Is . . .

Rubbish is junk that can give serious germs.
It is part of our school project.
It is a boy who has been to the fish and chip shop
throwing away his litter.
It is aluminium blowing in the ditch.
It is chewing gum stuck to your shoe.
It is crisp packets rustling in the street.
It is a bottle smashed and cutting wee one's fingers.
It is little girls and boys throwing apple cores.

Rachel Richardson (8)
St Andrew's RC Primary School, Gorebridge

Candle Burning

Candle burning, as orange and wobbly as
a huge punching bag.
Candle burning, as yellow and quickly
as a car zooming through the motorway.
Candle burning, as red and wobbly as a
slinky going down the narrow stairs.
Candle burning, as blue and wavy as the sea
violently comes in.
Candle burning, silent like a dark lonely room.
Candle burning, as peaceful as the calm, gentle
river, trickling on a hot summer's day.

Stephanie Napier (10)
St Andrew's RC Primary School, Gorebridge

Rubbish Is . . .

Rubbish is something that you can reduce, recycle and reuse.
It is chewing gum stuck to the boy's shoe.
It is wasting energy, throwing out rubbish.
It is trees getting made into flapping paper.
It is someone throwing rubbish down the dirty street.
It is teabags decomposting every two days.
It is a man picking up rubbish and putting it in
                                    the recycling box.
It is a man that is burning plastic.
It is a mouse that has been poisoned with some wine.
Rubbish is a lot of paper blowing in the wind.

Jed Baxter (9)
St Andrew's RC Primary School, Gorebridge

My Friend

He's a smart computer typing quickly.
He's an energetic lion patrolling the field.
He's the smell of a moist tree just been planted.
He's the sound of noisy laughter coming from
happy children.
He's the cold night's breeze cooling the night.
He's the warm summer's sun warming the day.
He's a bouncing jelly jumping on my plate.
He's the cool spring breeze blowing the trees.
He's a bright red cherry growing quickly.

Jamie Doherty (10)
St Andrew's RC Primary School, Gorebridge

My Mum

She's a love lightner
She's a peacemaker
She's a red rose
She's a child carer
She's a blood stopper
She's a super carer
She's a flowery leaf
She's a breakfast maker
She's a sunset
She's a porridge maker
Who is she? My mum that's who!

Ryan Russell (11)
St Andrew's RC Primary School, Gorebridge

Snow

The snowflakes fell silently like little pictures
falling on the floor.
The snow, like cotton wool, landed on the
ground while the children were laughing.
The snowman feeling cold and special stood
quietly in the snow.
The dripping wet slush was crunching while
people walked slowly over it.
The freezing ice reflected in the puddles as the
kids ran through them.
The crystal see-through icicle started shining
in the sunlight as the sun melted the snow
and made the kids shout.
Snowballs getting flung in every direction,
kids shouting, yelling and crying.

Heather Lyon (9)
St Andrew's RC Primary School, Gorebridge

My Friend

She's a warm bed on a cold, frosty day.
She's a soft cat curled up at the bottom of my feet.
She's a bright red rose shouting out in the garden.
She's the sound of a tweeting bird in the tree.
She's the sunrise of dawn.
She's a red-hot sunny day.
She's a sweet chocolate biscuit.
She's a burning summer sun.
She's an orange pencil drawing.

Lisa Loughrie (10)
St Andrew's RC Primary School, Gorebridge

My Mum

She's a red rose,
She's a homework helper,
She's a maths master,
She's a superstar,
She's a ball bouncer,
She's the sunset,
She's a magic mum,
She's a super speller
Who is it? My mum that's who!

Christopher Hogg (10)
St Andrew's RC Primary School, Gorebridge

My Mum

She's a bedmaker
She's a super driver
She's a blood stopper
She's a bathroom cleaner
She's a soup maker
She's a tea maker
She's a house cleaner
She's a brilliant mother.

Nathan Dalgleish (9)
St Andrew's RC Primary School, Gorebridge

My Friend

He's a prickly brush in a cupboard.
He's a fast speedy cheetah in the plains.
He's the smell of paint on the wall.
He's the quietness of a bird.
He's a bright ray of morning sunlight.
He's a bright red apple.
He's the spring blossom in the morning.
He's bright red.

Craig Tytler (10)
St Andrew's RC Primary School, Gorebridge

My Friend

She's a calculator counting quickly.
She's a beautiful butterfly fluttering in the sky.
She's a bright yellow daffodil standing tall.
She's a bright sun shining in the daylight sky.
She's a burning sun sparkling in the sky.
She's a lovely ripe strawberry ready to be picked.
She's a lovely flower sprung in spring.
She's a bright flaming ball of fire like the big
Shining sun burning in the sky.

Rachel Napier (10)
St Andrew's RC Primary School, Gorebridge

My Friend

She's a bright light standing in the corner.
She's a puppy begging on the doorstep.
She's the smell of a tulip in the garden.
She's the sound of a miaowing kitten.
She's the bright morning sky on a summer's day.
She's the sun shining in the sky.
She's a hairy sweetie in the cupboard.
She's summer with birds in the blue sky.
She's the colour of baby pink in my bedroom.

Lauren Jardine (10)
St Andrew's RC Primary School, Gorebridge

A Week Of Winter Weather

On Monday the Arctic winds blew like a gust of blowing fans
in our faces.
On Tuesday the clouds were like floating tufts of wool in the sky.
On Wednesday the snow was like falling sugar from the sky.
On Thursday the frost was like gold and silver glitter
sprinkled everywhere.
On Friday the rain was like pouring water in a glass.

Matthew Duncan (9)
St Peter's Primary School, Edinburgh

A Week Of Winter Weather

On Monday there were Arctic winds like a giant
With his fan blowing all his cold air on us;
Like an army charging at us
With their cold swords stabbing our cheeks.

On Tuesday it was cloudy
As if burnt marshmallows were covering the sky.
Like two giant gloved hands;
Floating in front of the lovely bright moon.

On Wednesday it was snowing
As if a giant was eating a white biscuit . . .
With all its crumbs falling onto the earth . . .
Or a boy sitting on a cloud pouring icing sugar on the world.

On Thursday it was frosty
Like frost giants blowing all their frosty breath on us . . .
Like a massive shiny crystal on the ground.

On Friday it was raining
Like a witch on her broomstick spitting on us . . .
Or a giant with a watering can pouring it on the land.

Gabriella Alonzi (10)
St Peter's Primary School, Edinburgh

A Week Of Wintry Weather

On Monday Arctic winds came charging in, from the north;
Ripping up the surrounding territory.
On Tuesday it clouded over, like great vast sheets
Engulfing the pale blue sky, daunting us with spits of rain.
On Wednesday it snowed, like hundreds of little cannon balls
Falling and transforming the world into a white sphere.
On Thursday it was frosty like a cover of cold crystal counterpane,
Nipping at our fingers and toes.
On Friday it rained as though the clouds had opened fire,
Making us wrap-up warm and return to our comforting homes.

David Cooper (9)
St Peter's Primary School, Edinburgh

A Week Of Winter Weather

On Monday,
The arctic winds were like a swarm of mischievous frost fairies
Trying to blind us.

On Tuesday,
The cloudy sky was as though the sun was abandoning the earth
To shine on another world.

On Wednesday,
The snow came down like snow fairies falling from heaven
On an errand to cover the world.

On Thursday,
The frost was like little white beings
Creeping over our summer's greens.

On Friday,
The rain came down like fireworks from the stars,
Their sparks fell and flooded our lands
And destroyed the bitter cold we had to cope with.

Luke Paxton (10)
St Peter's Primary School, Edinburgh

A Week Of Winter Weather

On Monday the Arctic winds came like an icy army,
Marching across the Atlantic Ocean.

On Tuesday the cloudy sky was a silvery grey blanket,
Hovering over the coldening sky.

On Wednesday the snow was like white pearls,
Descending from the heavens.

On Thursday the frost appeared like shining crystals,
Patterned on the ground.

On Friday the rain came
As if the Lord was weeping from the clouds.

Stuart Brown (9)
St Peter's Primary School, Edinburgh

A Week Of Winter Weather

On Monday the Arctic wind blew in from the north
Like howling frost giants;
Fighting, striking and piercing through the atmosphere.

On Tuesday, the clouds covered the sky;
Like a big gloved hand,
Covering the enormous sky, making it look like night.

On Wednesday, the snow came falling down;
Like doves flying to the ground,
Making the whole ground white.

On Thursday the frost came and covered the snow;
Like crystals evolving,
Making the ground crunchy.

On Friday, the horrendous rain came crashing down;
Like mini bombs falling on the frozen fortress;
Melting it away.

Patrick Burns (9)
St Peter's Primary School, Edinburgh

A Week Of Winter Weather

On Monday Arctic winds arrived like a fierce army
Charging towards us, blasting us with their sharp tongues.

On Tuesday cloudy balls of cotton wool filled the sky
With puffy white floating dots.

On Wednesday snow floated down,
Like rabbits tails dancing in a field of blue grass.

On Thursday frost appeared
Like crystals forming on lakes and window ledges,
Reflecting images like a mirror on the wall.

On Friday rain fell like giant tears,
Dripping and rolling with sadness, like a water slide that never ends.

Tayla Garrod (10)
St Peter's Primary School, Edinburgh

A Week Of Winter Weather

On Monday there were Arctic winds
Like huge frost giants appearing from nowhere,
Blowing their icy breath like a hairdryer for freezing.

On Tuesday it was cloudy
Like white gloves enveloping the blue sky,
Like lions coming in for the kill.

On Wednesday it was snowing,
Like pixies nationwide with their sugar dusters,
Sprinkling all around the country, covering it in snow.

On Thursday it was frosty
Like diamonds forming,
Making you wrap up warm and drink hot cocoa.

On Friday it was raining as though the clouds had opened fire,
Shooting any part of you that isn't covered up properly.

Thomas Gracie (10)
St Peter's Primary School, Edinburgh

A Week Of Winter Weather

On Monday Arctic winds,
Like frost giants blowing their icy breath over the land.

On Tuesday cloudy,
Like a fleet of grey candyfloss sailing across the sky.

On Wednesday snowy,
Like cotton wool descending gently from the sky
Forming a soft blanket on the ground.

On Thursday frosty,
Like huge sheet of transparent glass covering the roads.

On Friday rainy,
Like pails of water softly cascading onto the rooftops
Making a gentle tune.

Maria Luisa Iannone (10)
St Peter's Primary School, Edinburgh

A Week Of Winter Weather

On Monday
The Arctic winds charged in
Like a fierce army dashing into battle.

On Tuesday,
The clouds floated in
Like a thick grey blanket,
Wandering about the sky making us scamper into our houses.

On Wednesday,
The snow descended from the sky
Like icing sugar falling from the great heavens above.

On Thursday,
The frost arrived like gleaming crystals,
Sticking to everything in patterns.

On Friday,
The rain came like open fire,
Falling down from the sky, making us sprint to our houses.

Amber MacLeod (10)
St Peter's Primary School, Edinburgh

A Winter Poem

On Monday there were Arctic winds
Which blew in like an ice-cold breath moving across the earth.

On Tuesday there were clouds like a white blanket,
Overcastting the sky, and hiding the sun.

On Wednesday it was snowing,
Like ice-cold sugar falling from the sky, and onto the earth below.

On Thursday there was frost,
Like glass holding onto the earth; trying not to melt into water.

On Friday the rain arrived,
Like a knight charging on his horse, forcing us into our homes.

Ross Muir (9)
St Peter's Primary School, Edinburgh

A Week Of Winter Weather

On Monday Arctic winds came like frost giants charging
Like a fierce army freezing everything in their path.

On Tuesday cloudy, gloomy as a dark nightmare.

On Wednesday snowy, like a white blanket falling from the sky.

On Thursday frosty, like a glacial spike with an unwelcoming breeze.

On Friday rainy like a shower of rain hitting your head
As hard as it can, making you retreat to your homes.

Jamie Nicholson (9)
St Peter's Primary School, Edinburgh

Daisy

Daisy, Daisy, don't be lazy if I say that don't go crazy
Please Daisy, don't go crazy when you are picking a daisy
Milly, Milly, you're so silly and you're so very frilly
My little sister Milly wears a hat when it's chilly
Evie, Evie, you're so wheezy and also sneezy
What's the matter Evie? You're so rolled up and teeny
My name is Joseph and I like to play games
When I am angry I go up in hot flames.

Joseph Flucker (7)
St Peter's Primary School, Edinburgh

Summer

Summer is coming and the leaves are green,
The birds are playful and so are the bees.
But suddenly the rain falls
And all the animals run into their homes,
Lightning roams the forest, sounding like feet.
Then, all of a sudden
The sun pushes through and the rain goes away
And all of the animals come back out to play.

Ewan Feeney (12)
St Peter's Primary School, Edinburgh

A Week Of Winter Weather

On Monday Arctic winds were
Sticking spears in our faces
And hairdryers blasted cold air
On our bare legs and arms.

On Tuesday cloudy white sheep were covering the sky
And fluffy crystal candyfloss
Made castles and towers.

On Wednesday snow engulfed us
Like giants having pillow fights above
Then feathers landed softly below.

On Thursday frost descended on us
Like frost giants coming from below
And broke into little pieces.

On Friday rain was spitting
Like devils crying
And crystals came down hard.

Geraldine Gray (9)
St Peter's Primary School, Edinburgh

A Week Of Winter Weather

On Monday savage, wild dogs protecting their territory
From the outdoors.

On Tuesday two huge black gloved hands consuming the skies.

On Wednesday snow like two doves fluttering off into the world
Spreading peace.

On Thursday the placid frost sliding from the last leaf
Moving slowly but silently as the people walk past.

On Friday like the almighty God's tears falling
No one aware of His sorrow from the sad dark skies.

Michael Paterson (10)
St Peter's Primary School, Edinburgh

Changing

I have changed
By being prepared
And not being so
Scared

I just tried
And I never cried
All through Lagganlia
Camp

Back from Lagganlia
Learnt something new
What I thought I could not
Do

No more parents
Could I survive
But when I got there I was in for a
Surprise.

Eilidh McMillan (10)
St Peter's Primary School, Edinburgh

My Gran

I like my gran an awful lot.
She often cooks in a pot.
She can't drive a car.
But she walks fast and far.
She had a boy.
He is my dad.
Sometimes he goes a bit too mad!
My gran has some toys.
And some are for boys.
She has football games.
Her fire goes on flames!
Over there she has a gun.
Oh my gran's a lot of fun!

Daniel Pacitti (7)
St Peter's Primary School, Edinburgh

Jessica

Jessica is only one
She doesn't like to suck her thumb
Jessica is learning how to talk
And she's learning how to walk
She sometimes gets in moods with me
But she forgets it easily
She sometimes stands on the settee
And she always plays with me
Jessica sometimes wanders off
But we don't miss her a big lot!

Molly Donovan (7)
St Peter's Primary School, Edinburgh

My Cousin Reece

My cousin Reece will come in peace.
He wonders who will be his niece.
One day he might just give his fleece away.
Then his dad he will have to pay.
I think he will go to Greece for his holidays
To increase his football skills.
He is only six.
And still picks at his Twix.

Matthew Gormley (7)
St Peter's Primary School, Edinburgh

My Wee Sister Ellie

My wee sister is called Ellie.
My sister smiles when she watches telly
And I think her feet are smelly.
When she eats jelly it slips down her dress.
And then she screams as it hits her vest
Because she's in a mess.

Anna Service (7)
St Peter's Primary School, Edinburgh

Joe

I've got a little brother he is called Joe.
I am tall and he is low.
Joe likes to play in hay.
He never wants to go away.
He likes to play in the mud.
He never wears a pink hood.
He likes watching telly.
He loves eating jelly.
He likes to run around.
He doesn't like a very loud sound.

Tom Jarvis (7)
St Peter's Primary School, Edinburgh

My Sister Mhairi-Claire

I have a little sister and her name is Mhairi-Claire
And it's funny because I nick her underwear.
Mhairi-Claire is very cheeky
And very sneaky.
She will share
Before I dare.
She is so creepy
It makes her sleepy.
Mhairi-Claire likes to go to the fair
And she has fun in the air!

Charlotte McGowan (7)
St Peter's Primary School, Edinburgh

Cheetah - Haiku

A cheetah as fast
As the speed of light and soft
Patterned, dotted fur.

Adam Al Khateb (11)
St Peter's Primary School, Edinburgh

A Lagganlia Transformation

I went to Lagganlia
The fun adventure course
I did some cool activities
At dinner I could've eaten a horse

I had fun at Lagganlia
But I've now changed quite a bit
I've come back more responsible
And also very fit

I went to Lagganlia
And up the rocks I climbed
I overcame my fear
And had a really super time

Goodbye now Lagganlia
You've changed me quite a lot
I'm stronger and I'm braver
And Lagganlia,
You rock!

Catrina Randall (11)
St Peter's Primary School, Edinburgh

My Brother David

My brother David is only nine
And he cannot drink any wine.
He has bad manners when he goes to dine
One day by accident he swallowed a pine.
He always says 'I'm doing fine'
He says, 'No, I'll sign'
He also says, 'No, that's mine'
He can't stand still when he's in a line
When he sits he looks like he has no spine
But I sometimes like that brother of mine.

Eloise Cooper (7)
St Peter's Primary School, Edinburgh

My Pudding

Mum that's my strawberry tart,
Hey Dad, don't eat my chocolate cake,
It's mine, mine, mine.
Don't you dare touch that apple strudel,
Donald don't think about eating my banana flan,
It's mine, mine, mine.
You don't touch my giant chocolate cookie,
Don't go near my ice cream,
It's mine, mine, mine.
Touch my ice cream float and I'll be angry,
Don't think about eating my chocolate profiteroles,
They're mine, mine, mine.
Crunch!
Hey!

Anna Ghazal (11)
St Peter's Primary School, Edinburgh

Laila

Laila is so very cute.
Laila likes to hold her foot.
Laila likes to suck her thumb.
While she's snuggling into Mum.
Laila always pulls my hair
Which isn't very fair.
She looks at me
When I'm eating my tea.
She wakens and sings,
In the mornings.

Lucia Corace (7)
St Peter's Primary School, Edinburgh

My Gran

My gran's a nice wee nan.
She is quite brown, she has a tan.

My gran is careful of what she wears.
She doesn't like apples, she really likes pears.

She has some hairs up her nose.
Her favourite flower is a rose.

Sometimes she is happy, sometimes she is sad.
Sometimes she shouts at me that makes me mad.

She has short grey hair
But she doesn't care.

Anya Macsorley Pringle (7)
St Peter's Primary School, Edinburgh

A Week Of Winter Weather

On Monday Arctic winds are charging
Like a fierce army battling and whistling on the earth.

On Tuesday cloudy
Like a flock of sheep galloping round in the sky.

On Wednesday, the snow appeared as if
A great frost giant was eating white chocolate cookies
And the crumbs were falling through the sky.

On Thursday frost arrived
Like diamonds forming from nowhere.

On Friday, the rain descended as if a baby giant was crying
And tears were falling from heaven.

Lesley Wong (10)
St Peter's Primary School, Edinburgh

Transformation

Lagganlia was so much fun
Even though I had to run
Through the woods and up the hills
Down the gorge with its thrills and spills

The view was good the room was great
I made good friends with my roommates
And keeping the room so nice and clean
Till it shone so well with a shiny sheen

But Lagganlia made me change
From a huge big lazy pain
To responsible independent Matty G
Team player extraordinaire.

Matthew Gallagher (10)
St Peter's Primary School, Edinburgh

A Week Of Winter Weather

On Monday fierce Arctic winds
Like competitive eagles flapping their wings to make a wind.

On Tuesday evil clouds
Like fumes escaping from a gas station.

On Wednesday white snow
Like cotton wool falling from the sky.

On Thursday scary frost giants
Freezing us with their bodies.

On Friday joyful rain
Like a knight fighting back with a lance.

Graham Goode (10)
St Peter's Primary School, Edinburgh

I Am Changed

The air was fresh
The air was sweet
As I heard the sound
Of pattering feet.

Here come the staff
As we tremble off the coach
Trying to suss the instructors
As they approach.

As quick as a blink
We were all back in school
Chatting and gabbing
Lagganlia was cool.

I feel more independent
A go for it kid
I have more experience
I loved it, yes I did.

I am now more responsible
In each and every way
But hang on just a minute
I have something to say.

Thanks Mum and Dad
Thanks Mrs Blair
You have transformed me
But my body is sair.

Danielle Cathro (10)
St Peter's Primary School, Edinburgh

Acorn

Small little acorn,
Falling from the tree so high,
Lying on the ground.
You sink down into the earth,
Growing to become a tree.

Ruth Robertson (11)
St Peter's Primary School, Edinburgh

Changing

I spent a week in Lagganlia
I've changed a lot since then
I had great fun and learnt
A lot of different things ye ken

Before I went my mum would say
'Your bedroom is a mess'
But now I'm back I've learned to keep it
Untidy less and less

The first day I went climbing
That worried me a lot
But as the week went on and on
My confidence grew hot

And that was not just climbing
New watersports as well
Cycling through the forest
Up the tree to ring the bell

I had to be responsible
For my kit throughout the week
And helpful to my colleagues
Being cheerful not a geek

And teamwork was important
Which I now understand
I've learned a lot in Lagganlia
Now I will always lend a hand.

William Reeves (11)
St Peter's Primary School, Edinburgh

Tanka

Fireworks are speeding
Flies hyper high, like bullets
Fountain bang and boom!
Swirly ones and rockets, too
It makes beautiful patterns.

Blair Donaldson (11)
St Peter's Primary School, Edinburgh

The Flying Pig

One day, I looked into the sky,
And guess what I saw flying by?
It was pink and looked really big,
Oh my goodness, it was a pig!

I never knew that pigs could fly,
Way up high in the bright blue sky.
Well maybe that is all so true,
Way up there in the sky so blue.

Emma McGachie (10)
St Peter's Primary School, Edinburgh

I've Grown Up

Things are different today
I'm different from before
I'm doing things another way
I've grown up some more

I'm feeling really friendly
I'm different from before
No more of me being deadly
I've grown up some more.

Anne Cameron (10)
St Peter's Primary School, Edinburgh

Space

Some objects live in space
That must be stars -
Or planets.
I might to go space . . .
To sit on the galaxies
And see all the stars.

Sang Hee Lee (11)
St Peter's Primary School, Edinburgh

Transformation

It became quite clear
When I arrived home
From exciting Lagganlia

The difference in me
Was very nice to see
After creative Lagganlia

A mature young lady
So willing to help
During wonderful Lagganlia

Home with my family
Mature and alert
Thank you Lagganlia.

Dominique Charleston (11)
St Peter's Primary School, Edinburgh

Transformed

I went to Lagganlia
Full of cheer
I had to be brave
And face my fear
Long cold days
Full of fun
It would have been nice
To have some sun
On my return
A brand new me
Ever so pleased
To see my family.

Justin Hepburn (12)
St Peter's Primary School, Edinburgh

Supreme

Coming back from Lagganlia
How it has changed me
Tidier and cleaner
What will they all say?

Taking responsibility
For more and more things
Mum says 'Stop skiving'
But I just start to sing

Getting on with people
Working as a team
Listening to instructors
It has been supreme.

Charlotte Dick (11)
St Peter's Primary School, Edinburgh

The Good Me

I am an angel most of the time
But I transformed when I was nine
At home I'm often a great big horror
Especially to Mum, Dad and poor little brother

To all of my teachers I'm the girl who's OK
But that is for show while we're in the school day
Because my horns come out and the good me drops
I rant and I rave and I go in a strop

When I am in bed the horror's away
And the angel comes back to start a new day
The transformation is there all new and complete
For the next day when me and Mrs Blair meet.

Courtney Kyle (11)
St Peter's Primary School, Edinburgh

Improving

When I was at camp
I never listened much
Now I always listen
To what the teacher says

I never used to try things
Now I always do
Even if I'm scared
I always try to do

I never was responsible
Now I always am
I take responsibility
For everything that's mine.

Callum Kerr (10)
St Peter's Primary School, Edinburgh

Back From Lagganlia

Arriving home from Lagganlia
I said 'Hi Mum, it's good to see ya!'
I've grown up a lot and learned to make my bed
But I'd rather leave it to my mum instead.

While I was there I learned to make lunch
Miss Thomson even gave us a biscuit to munch
I am more responsible, reliable too
Now my mum will always give me tasks to do

Me and my friends have learned a load
Danielle even held a toad
We learned to work and play together
And built friendships that will last forever.

Daniela Cernicchiaro (10)
St Peter's Primary School, Edinburgh

No More Worry

Before I went to Lagganlia
I was worried about leaving my family
But now I have changed
After Lagganlia.

I was scared to climb the tree so high
I was scared to skywalk in the sky
But now I have changed
After Lagganlia.

Since I have been to Lagganlia
I have become a little bit more tidy
And more responsible since I have
Been to Lagganlia.

Sophie Dolan (11)
St Peter's Primary School, Edinburgh

Sports Day

Sports day is great!
Running in silly clothes - going mad!
Throwing the javelin
Really high so it
Will touch the sky
Bouncing that basketball
Around the court
Kicking the football
Through the cones
Making a racket
Is that fun or what!

Ava Pullar (11)
St Peter's Primary School, Edinburgh

Fairytales

Once I opened up my book,
And I saw a confusing picture.
I called to my mother, 'Look Mum, look!
Look at this fairytale mixture.'

Cinderella's prince was now a frog,
And no princess was there to kiss him.
Spells backfired, from butlers to dog,
And there was a beautiful sister that was smart, not dim.

Hansel and Gretel had no bread,
The witch's house was made of wood.
'Oh no, this story's all wrong!' they said,
'We would turn back time if we could!'

The fairies forgot about Sleeping Beauty's christening,
They turned up late with no gifts at all.
When the king gave a speech, the guests were not listening,
And the witch did not attend the eighteenth-birthday ball.

Snow White could not find the dwarf's house;
She got lost in the forest instead!
She was scared at even the sight of a mouse,
And the prince came down with the flu, a cough and a rather
                                        sore head!'

My mother was really quite confused,
She sighed and shook her head.
My father was amazed and amused,
And that night I dream of frogs, the flu, gifts and sore heads!

Keira O'Sullivan Robertson (10)
St Peter's Primary School, Edinburgh

Haiku

The tree groaned as it
Fell. It was so horrible
It fell with a crash!

Owen Mooney (10)
St Peter's Primary School, Edinburgh

A Weird Dog

I know a dog, his name is Brandy,
He eats everything, especially candy!

Once I took him for a walk,
He pulled on his lead,
And just wouldn't let me talk.

So I invited my friend round to tea,
Brandy went mad, started chasing a bee,
He's a bad dog, don't you agree?

Summertime, off to Spain,
Brandy wanted to come, he was being such a pain.
So I took him to Spain,
Typical, it was pouring with rain.

At the hotel I met a friend,
Brandy kept barking,
He was driving me round the bend!

Back in Scotland, in the house,
Brandy thought he saw a mouse.

Let me tell you . . .
Brandy he's the best,
Better than the rest,
Even though he can be a pest!

Hope Thompson (11)
St Peter's Primary School, Edinburgh

Tanka

Night sky was so black
Until - suddenly *bang! Bang!*
Bang! The sky lit up
With mystic sparks red, blue, green
Leaves behind a smoky cloud.

Kealan Delaney (10)
St Peter's Primary School, Edinburgh

School Life

Red shirt, blue top, yellow house,
Feeling as small as a mouse,
Tracing C in the sand,
Teachers holding my hand,
Language and maths,
Break at half past,
Homework and studies,
With all of my best buddies,
No toys and games,
Saying you're lame,
Normal and goth,
'Oh bug off'
Last day of school
Going in the pool,
Yes, oh whoa
I'll see you soon.

Morag Williams (10)
Sciennes Primary School, Edinburgh

Jaguars

Jaguars are great,
Except when they take the bait,
They pounce very fast.
Fast, sleek and deadly,
Except when they are asleep,
Eating when they can.
They pounce very fast,
Killing a lot in long grass,
Eating when they kill.

Kirstie-Ann McPherson & Rebecca Thomason (10)
Sciennes Primary School, Edinburgh

The Last Day Together!

Beep! Beep! Beep!
It was Charlie Strong's mobile,
A reminder! The last day of school!
She got up, and went to the bathroom,
Put on the tap, the water was cool.

After her bath, she was clean as a whistle,
She got dressed for the school day ahead of her,
She walked along the landing,
Where her cat Morag, gave a purr!

On her way to school,
She thought to herself, with a sigh,
'When I get there I will soon have to say goodbye!'

The nine o'clock bell rang, ding, ding, ding,
It was time to go into class,
It was the geometry test!
'Oh please, oh please let me pass!'

After the test it was time for lunch,
Stew, *yuck!* She thought.
The teacher made an announcement,
'You're all good pupils I've taught!'

It was time for PE class,
Rounders was last on the list!
Charlie was chosen to bat,
But every time she missed!

It was time for the party,
Everyone was going to be there!
There was music, dancing and all that stuff
But no one really did dare.

People were sad, some happy,
Some in their hearts felt pain,
Then behind Charlie came a voice,
'We'll never see each other again!'

The voice belonged to a boy,
His name, Carlos Tiss,
He was devoted to Charlie,
And that day ended with a kiss!

Karis McKechnie (11)
Silverwood Primary School, Kilmarnock

Last Day

Last day at Silverwood,
Most primary seven are sad, others are filled with joy.
I am standing alone,
Memories fill my head,
Then, I am filled with dread
Of the new school.
Stupid!
I've been on the induction day
I've seen what it is like
It's not bad.
Everything is big enough
The hall's wide enough,
The playground large enough,
The PE equipment harder to use.
Now I am excited, about the move,
So many new things,
But, it will never be the same,
Will it?

Daniel King (12)
Silverwood Primary School, Kilmarnock

The Last Day

The last day of school
The last day of primary
The junior sports day.

I don't want to leave school,
I want this day to never end,
The teacher called my class to get into line.
All my friends run to line
But not me, I couldn't.

I was the only one left
I couldn't move my body
I wanted to do it all again.

The teacher called me in
I didn't want to
I would lose my vice badge
I would lose my responsibility.

Darren Brown (12)
Silverwood Primary School, Kilmarnock

Last Day Of School

Oh no! Last day, then it's summer holidays.
What if people bully me?
What if I don't fit in?
What if?
I'm so scared, but so excited!
I will get to be so organised
I can't wait.
Then again, what if no one likes me?
What if no one wants to be my friend?
It's all in my imagination it will be great!
Now, don't worry.
Go and play, relax, just enjoy being in primary
While it lasts!

Emma-Lee Kelso (12)
Silverwood Primary School, Kilmarnock

Leaving School

The thought passes my mind,
I'm leaving this behind.
For better or for worse,
That's what the teacher said.

The good times and the bad,
The happy and the sad,
All these things fly through my head
But then the teacher said;

'Wake up, wake up!
You're not at home yet!'
Another half hour left
Of my primary school life.

Fifteen minutes later,
The teacher still droning on
The children getting restless
As the last day trundles on.

The end of the day,
A big *hooray!*
As we walk out singing,
I think about the future.

Secondary school
Just seems so scary,
I've heard about it
From my mum and
It sounds quite mean.

Oh well, I am a wee bit keen!
New teachers, new friends
And a new beginning.

Mikey Reynolds (11)
Silverwood Primary School, Kilmarnock

Back To School Reality

Brrring!
The three o'clock bell,
Only fifteen minutes to go.
The very last day until I move
I hope these last minutes go slow.

I think of the great times
Good and bad,
That have happened in seven years.
And then I know I'll have to leave,
And my eyes are filled with tears.

The netball team, dinner monitors,
The trip to New Lanark and stuff.
Leaving Silverwood this year
Will be sad and tough.

Come on Becca, it's not that bad,
Think what's ahead of you,
New friends, new teachers, a few nice boys,
Everything's gonna be new!

'Becca, Becca why aren't you away?
It's almost twenty past three!
Unless you would like to stay behind,
And tidy up with me!'

I got up, packed my bag,
And put away my chair,
I picked up my coat, walked to the door,
And I looked back for one more stare.

That's it, that's all I get,
Just one chance to remember.
Oh my gosh, what will I be like,
In first year next December.

It's the first day of a new term
And oh I'm already late,
This is just fabulous
Secondary life isn't it just great!

Man oh man, I don't believe it,
I've forgotten my homework again!
'Rebecca Shawn, it's not good enough
You are always the same!'

Hometime, phew! We can't get out quick enough,
Secondary's harder than it looks,
Really it's quite tough!

Jodie McMonagle (12)
Silverwood Primary School, Kilmarnock

Bye-Bye Silverwood!

I sit and think as the clock reaches two-twenty-five,
The last day of school is meant to be a happy day,
But not for me!
Everyone else is playing board games, as happy as could be.

I will miss the bright-coloured pictures hanging on the wall,
And the way we lined up, small to tall.
I will miss going to netball, after school,
And going swimming at the Galleon's pool
The fun I had, the games I played.
I wish I could just stay!

I am so upset, I don't want to go.
Induction days went in so slow!
The James Hamilton is so big,
Too big for me.
At Silverwood I felt big, but now I feel so wee!

Nicole Phillips (12)
Silverwood Primary School, Kilmarnock

Sports Day

The crowds are cheering, making a din,
I've just been in a race, but I didn't win.
Now I'm up again, for another run,
There's a cool breeze, and I'm having fun.
The whistle blows,
The crowd goes,
I run towards the finish line,
Someone fell, I heard a whine.
The finish line is nearly there,
It's finished now, back to my chair.

Now it's time for another race,
I wipe the sweat off my face.
The crowd are cheering once again,
All the women, children and men.
The race is won by another boy,
My mum and brother with his toy
Are cheering in the crowd,
I know my mum'll be proud.
Now it's all done,
We can relax in the summer sun.
Mrs Clark is making a speech,
That is a lesson she could teach.

Now it's time to go home for tea,
It's the last Wednesday here I'll ever see.
Now I'm ready to go home,
Then outside, I will roam.

Jason Murphy (11)
Silverwood Primary School, Kilmarnock

Silverwood Football Team

The last day
Of the last week
Of the last month.

I never wanted this to end,
I thought my name would never get called out,
I was excited, but sad because it was the last day.
My name, my name
Oh alleluia, out of class at last
I can't wait!

But I'll miss the lessons
Miss the lessons, who cares?
I'll be playing for the school not just writing for it.

The trials, I'll miss them if I don't shut up
Ready, at last, I'm ready to play.

It's over, I'm picked
Picked; I can't believe it,
Playing for the school team
I am so proud.

I'm not sad, I'll be playing in this magnificent place,
I will always loved this school.

The bell has just rung and the last day is over
James Hamilton here I come,
But I leave Silverwood with pride.

Stuart Johnstone (11)
Silverwood Primary School, Kilmarnock

Last Time

Reading, silent reading for the last time,
Last day of school,
The last lesson I'll ever have.

The words don't make sense anymore
Squashed together like us in our tiny classroom,
The blackboard creaking in the cramped corner.

We're going to big school soon,
Soon! Not soon enough,
Those teachers make our lives too tough.

Someone just nudged my back,
The bell has gone, no turning back the clock,
I run out of the classroom.
No! This is all wrong
I can't go to big school!
Having to start again, it's not fair.

Fair! Nothing's fair I have to live with it
Live with it! I have to live with everything.

I tossed my head back and walked through the gate
For the last time.

Jodie Neilson (11)
Silverwood Primary School, Kilmarnock

Last Day

It's my last day of primary school
I'm really going round the bend
Because secondary school doesn't look so cool,
But hey, I might make a new friend.

All my friends are going away,
And it's scary for most.
They're all going away today,
But there is no need to boast.

If your friends aren't going anywhere,
You may be happy or sad,
But you should just take a second to stop and stare
If you feel sad you should feel bad.

You should be glad not bad or sad,
'Cause you're growing up
But don't go mad
You'll soon be just like your mum or dad.

I don't want to move school
As you probably know,
I can't look a fool
I can't go, I won't go,
Or will I?

Emma Rae (11)
Silverwood Primary School, Kilmarnock

Silverwood Netball Team

The last day
Of the last term
Of primary seven.

It's the day before the summer holidays
I never wanted it to end
On a hot and sunny day.

I'm in the playground playing netball
With my teacher and all my friends
I thought I heard my name being called out but it wasn't.

This new school which I'm going to
I wonder what it's like
I will get new friends and all
New teachers and classes too.

Anyway I'd better concentrate on the game
I run, I catch the ball
Then I throw it right away.

The other person misses it
I have to go and get the ball.

I am going to miss this school
And all of the teachers too
Also this new school I'm going to
I'm excited to see you.

Jennifer Wilson (12)
Silverwood Primary School, Kilmarnock

The Last Day Of School

I'm Alasdair MacDonald of Tobermori Mull,
And it's my last day of primary school
I'm going to Mull High School
In August.

Looking back I've got into trouble more times than
The Earth's done a revolution since God made it,
Maybe that's because I'm as quiet as a rock group
That never stops rocking.

My most outrageous prank was putting a frog
In Miss MacStricklady's tea
Or maybe replacing Mr Hardmarine's water with urine,
They both won me my nickname 'Awful All'

Well, I do suppose I was talented in some subjects
Particularly history, modern studies and ICT,
I got some excellent reports
Particularly, from Mrs Goodmanne in Year Three.

Oh how many memories I have in this school
Both as prankster and an intelligent young man,
Oh how much change I've been through in seven years
And now I'm leaving.

I'm kind of looking forward to Mull High school,
I live so near it I practically live there!
My big brother tells me bad things about the school
But my best friend tells me they're all false.

Gavin McLaughlin (11)
Silverwood Primary School, Kilmarnock

School Is Finishing

The last day of school,
The last time I'll set foot in this class,
The last time I'll play in the playground,
The last time I'll walk down the corridor into the big hall,
The last time I'll do any of these things.

Sure I'm sad about leaving, but I've had a great time here.
When I go to secondary I know I'll have nothing to fear
Leaving will be like taking a part of me away
The more I think about secondary the more I think I don't
                                       want to stay.

I'm looking forward to my Induction Day,
I'll looking forward to seeing inside secondary school.
I've had a lot of ups and downs here in super Silverwood
I've become a vice captain for Dean,
I've become part of the media club and I've become a mentor,
And it makes me feel good knowing I've done something
                                       to leave behind,
But now it's time to move on.

Aaron Graham (11)
Silverwood Primary School, Kilmarnock

My Last Day At Silverwood

It is the very last day of my primary life,
Tomorrow is the summer holidays.

It is the last Easter competition
I am so disappointed,
I am also happy, I won in my class
My egg was as good as gold
And as pretty as a picture!

I will never get to do this again!
That will be a shame,
I will never get to do sports day either!
I'm good at sports.

The excitement of meeting new friends,
Frightened of new teachers,
Happiness of a new school!

I can't believe this day has come,
Like a jet plane flying through the sky!
It has come so quickly
I didn't even notice!

Well, we have to move on!
This is it!
The big day has come!

Shelby Hollas (11)
Silverwood Primary School, Kilmarnock

My Last Day

It is the last day
Of the seventh year
In primary school
And it's sports day.

The teacher called my class up
To race in the one hundred metres sprint
As she calls us up
My heart is racing faster and faster.

It's the last day of primary school
And the last sports day so I will make
The most of it. The gun went off
And we shot away.

I am pulling away from the
Others and the finishing line is
Becoming closer and closer.
I suddenly reached it and I won!
I won!

'Pack your bags now children,
The bell has just rung.' said the teacher
Secondary school here I come!
I'm glad I won at the sports
Day and I can't wait to
Go to secondary school.

Scott Jamieson (11)
Silverwood Primary School, Kilmarnock

Silverwood Vs James Hamilton

All my friends that seven years made stay,
Will all just drift away.
These seven years at Silverwood,
Have been the best they ever could.
The teachers, bad and good, watched us grow,
And put up with us, even though.
Today when we say goodbye
My friends and I would try not to cry.
Most of the people we know,
Will all cheer when we go!

The James Hamilton, scary stuff,
Will just appear in a puff.
All those corridors and all those rooms,
The classrooms will feel like tombs!
Then there's the people we won't all know,
The teachers that we don't know won't
Have time to watch us grow
And now I'll be the baby.
It feels like it's my birthday party, 'cause
I'm all excited,
But I'll need to wait, to see, if I'm invited. . .

Kari Todd (12)
Silverwood Primary School, Kilmarnock

The End Of Primary Life

It was the last day of school,
And the day was really cool,
When I tried to beat the sports day record.

I hope I would win sports day,
Even if I didn't I would still be happy,
I wanted to be the winner.

I won the long jump,
And the high jump too,
The pentathlon
I pulled through.

It was the last event,
It was the ball throw,
I was drawing with my friend on the points chart,
I threw the ball,
It got to fifty and going further still,
It stopped at eighty-five,
Then my friend threw it,
It was at sixty as it started to go down,
It was at seventy-five, it got to eighty and stopped,
I jumped up in celebration, I had won!

Christopher Barbour (11)
Silverwood Primary School, Kilmarnock

The Beginning

It's an end of an era,
I have had the last dance at the disco,
I have thrown the last ball at sports day,
I have been down the last duty monitoring,
I have been hit on the head with a football for the last time,
It's all been done.
I am leaving primary school,
I will have to give in my house badge,
I will probably lose some of my friends,
Face it, it's over!
Maybe this is a good thing
Who knows what's in store for me,
Better discos,
More games on sports day
Shorter duties monitoring
Never been hit on the head with a football again!
Even maybe new friends,
So it's not really over,
It's just a new beginning.

Hannah McGill (12)
Silverwood Primary School, Kilmarnock

Summer Senses

At summer I think of going to the beach.
I'd get a suntan and I wouldn't come back peach.
I think of my cat lazing in the sun.
I hope he doesn't get sunburn.
I see sunflowers swaying in the breeze.
Butterflies flutter and so do bees.

I feel so happy when the sun comes out.
I can play outside all day, run and shout.

Eva Mitchell (9)
Stenhousemuir Primary School, Stenhousemuir

Summer Sun

Do you think of beaches when summer is near?
Hot summer sun, hot summer sun.
Holidays are in my head from here to here.

I see the bright sunshine glistening.
Hot summer sun, hot summer sun.
Dragonflies, butterflies and ladybirds too
All relaxing in the summer sun.

I feel happy and excited in summer
Hot summer sun, hot summer sun.
I relax in the summer, do you?
Summer has ended, time to say bye-bye.

Mairi Mackellaig (8)
Stenhousemuir Primary School, Stenhousemuir

Summer

I think of the beach when it is warm.
People shooting water pistols at each other.
Children wait for the summer fayre all day long,
I think of flowers.

I hear the sound of birds singing.
People laughing and shouting.
I hear the sound of horses neighing.
The sea crashing.

I see the wasps buzzing on the beach.
I pick some nice flowers.
I see topless boys
I see butterflies.

Chelcie MacKay (8)
Stenhousemuir Primary School, Stenhousemuir

The Summer Season

I think of holiday fun,
It's fun to play in the sun,
I know it is summer soon,
Hot summer sun.

I see wasps flying, butterflies too,
Water pistol fights,
Birds flying so softly,
Hot summer sun.

I hear bees humming,
People playing,
Waves splashing at the seaside,
Summer is great!

Mychaela Mealey (8)
Stenhousemuir Primary School, Stenhousemuir

Summer

I think of holiday fun and flowers.
I feel joyful and cheered up.
I smell roses and barbecues smelling tasty
And the grass might make you sneeze
Atishoo!

I hear birds singing sweetly
And bees buzzing and horses neighing
And people shouting and the sea waves are crashing!

I see water pistols and water bombs being fired and thrown about
I'm going home now, see you later, goodbye.

Graeme Wardrope (8)
Stenhousemuir Primary School, Stenhousemuir

Summer

I think of beaches when it is summer
Water gun fights cool you down,
Summer fayre is coming
So be ready.

I smell roses and flowers,
The barbecue smells lovely and tasty,
Grass being cut is a sneezing smell,
The sea is a beautiful smell.

I see the wasps buzzing,
I see the water pistols fighting,
The happy families rush to the airport,
There are midges all over.

Daniel Sharp (8)
Stenhousemuir Primary School, Stenhousemuir

Summer

I think of the summer sun
And the holiday that
We get and the sand on the beach
And the sun.

I hear birds singing,
And buzzing bees,
People out loud.

I feel excited about,
The summer coming,
And I feel relaxed!

Floyd Kesson (8)
Stenhousemuir Primary School, Stenhousemuir

Summer

I think of beaches when it is summer
Wasps, bees and dragonflies
Flying about the salty water.

I smell the grass being cut
And chicken being roasted and flowers.

I hear birds singing,
Bees buzzing and people laughing.
Summer, summer, summer.

Gary Grugen (8)
Stenhousemuir Primary School, Stenhousemuir

Summer Senses

I think of summer because it is warm and beautiful
And the sea is lovely.
I think it's wonderful and exciting.

I hear people playing outside having water gun fights
And playing in their paddling pool and jumping in.

I see butterflies fluttering by like a fan
And bees collecting honey and rabbits playing.
I love summer!

David Clark (8)
Stenhousemuir Primary School, Stenhousemuir

Summer Senses

I think of the summer holidays,
I think of the summer fayre.

I hear birds singing and bees buzzing,
People laughing and waves crashing.

I see butterflies flying beautifully,
I feel happy on a summer's day.

Ryan Miller (8)
Stenhousemuir Primary School, Stenhousemuir

Summer Senses

Hot summer sun, hot summer sun
In the lovely hot air.
I feel so happy I feel like I'm going to faint,
I love summer.

I think of summer when the flowers grow
And birds are singing happily up high.
I hear waves crashing on top of the sea
And people playing on the beach.

Hot summer sun, hot summer sun,
With sunshine brightly in the sky
And birds singing up high.

Ashley Harrower (9)
Stenhousemuir Primary School, Stenhousemuir

Summer Sun

I hear beautiful singing of the gold crest
People joyfully playing
Hot summer sun, hot summer sun.

I think of the beautiful beach and the sea crashing on the rocks,
I love the summer fayre,
Hot summer sun, hot summer sun.

I feel exhausted, sweaty and tried
When I have been playing in the sun
All day with my friends,
Hot summer sun, hot summer sun.

Jack Mitchell (8)
Stenhousemuir Primary School, Stenhousemuir

Summer Time

When I think of summer
I think of holidays and the nice warm sun.
I think of the beach as well with the blue sea and the soft warm sand.

In the summer
I hear children shouting and playing
And adults talking and laughing and I hear lots of buzzing bees.

I smell nice barbecues and people cutting their grass.
I smell the sunflower and the bright red roses
I also smell the blue sea.
I love summer!

Bronia Black (9)
Stenhousemuir Primary School, Stenhousemuir

Summer Sun

I think of the warm summer sun when it is near summer
Water fights and fun in the hot summer sun.

I feel happy, joyful and relaxed
I feel hot and sweaty too
I feel like I am going to explode with excitement
In the hot summer sun.

I see buzzing bumblebees
I see birds chirping in the sky
I see butterflies flying with their beautiful wings
In the hot summer sun.

Abbie Wishart (9)
Stenhousemuir Primary School, Stenhousemuir

Summer

I hear the buzzing bees
The birds sing so sweetly on hot summer days
People laugh so loud it's lovely to hear.

I smell the tasty barbecues on a light night
You can smell the brand new grass
The smell of the sea so salty.

In the summer I feel so excited
I get hot and burnt, 'Ow!' I say
I am so relaxed sunbathing
I am so joyful when it is summer.

Eva Brookes (8)
Stenhousemuir Primary School, Stenhousemuir

Summer

I think of water gun fights when it is summer
People playing on the beach
But best of all no school for six weeks.

I hear people shouting,
Birds singing so sweetly
Bees buzzing about collecting pollen from flowers.

I see lots of water guns and water bombs being thrown
Soaked boys with their tops off
And hotdogs to eat after the fun day.

Callum Cochrane (8)
Stenhousemuir Primary School, Stenhousemuir

Summer

I think of the summer fayre on summer days
I think of beaches in summer
Beaches in summer
Beaches in summer.

I hear birds singing in summer
Birds singing in summer
Birds singing in summer
I hear bees buzzing.

I feel burnt in summer
Burnt in summer
Burnt in summer
I am tired and exhausted after that long day.

Jordan Thomson (8)
Stenhousemuir Primary School, Stenhousemuir

Summer

What do you see in summer?
I see panting dogs on walks
And butterflies flying in the breeze
Also buzzing wasps in the sky.

I hear birds singing in the trees
Also buzzing bees collecting pollen from flowers
The noise of people laughing sounds just great.

How do you feel in summer?
I feel relaxed
Also I feel happy sitting in the sun
I love summer - it's great

Caitlyn Blues (8)
Stenhousemuir Primary School, Stenhousemuir

The Summer Season

I think off the shining sun when summer returns
Water gun fights are one of the best in summer
The summer fayre at school is brill as well.
In summer the flowers are so colourful.

I see bees buzzing in the flowers, searching for pollen
There are thousands of birds chirping away in the sunset sky
And best of all happy families laughing and smiling.

I smell the fab taste of yummy barbecues
I also smell the hayfever grass that makes me sneeze all the time
Best of all I can smell the lovely smell of summer roses
Summer is great!

Charlie Thomson (8)
Stenhousemuir Primary School, Stenhousemuir

Summer

In the summer I think of all the beautiful flowers
And getting buried in the sand at the beach
Plus we go to the summer fayre
Come along and win some things.

We hear the beautiful birds' sweet singing
When I go to my grandad's I hear the horses neighing.

I feel really excited in the summer
And it is fun to play in the pool with my friends.
Summer is fandabidose!

Monica Caie (8)
Stenhousemuir Primary School, Stenhousemuir

Summer Sense

When it's summer I love the wonderful holidays that you go on
I think the sun is very brilliant
I love summer, yeah!

I smell grass being cut it's a very strong smell
The barbecues smell lovely and tasty
And the roses have a wonderful smell
I love summer, yeah!

I feel really happy when summer is here
I'm completely relaxed sunbathing
I feel sweaty when it's hot
I love summer, it's great!

Justin Laurie (8)
Stenhousemuir Primary School, Stenhousemuir

Summer

When it comes to summer I think of holidays
Think of hot summer sun
And playing happily at the beach.

I hear the sweet birds singing
I hear the buzzing bees
All I hear in summer is people laughing and shouting.

I smell the barbecues which is lovely and tasty
The smell of a beautiful sunflower
I smell the grass being cut (a very awful smell).
I love summer - it's great!

Keira Morrison (8)
Stenhousemuir Primary School, Stenhousemuir

Summer

Summer makes me think of the beach and holidays
I like having water guns and water bomb fights.

I like the smell of my dad's flowers
That he planted in our front garden, they smell great.

Sometimes I feel bored
And sometimes I feel excited
But I still like summer.
Summer is great!

Grant Robertson (8)
Stenhousemuir Primary School, Stenhousemuir

Happiness

H appiness brings joy to all.
A nd brings out all the kindness in people.
P lease make people happy.
P eople will thank you for making them happy.
I n everyone there is happiness somewhere.
N o looking for a fight.
E ven if you are angry.
S tart off by finding joy.
S oon everyone will be happy.

Chelsea Blacklaw (9)
Tinto Primary School, Biggar

Biggar

B iggar is big but not too big
I nside every house it is warm.
G reat people live there.
G reat shops as well.
A pple trees are around.
R abbits live in the park.

Jenny Bruce (8)
Tinto Primary School, Biggar

Anger

Anger is a red blade,
It smells like fire.
Anger tastes like a boiling pit of lava.
It feels like a sharp edge hitting your side.
Anger lives in the heart of war.

Samantha Taylor (12)
Whitecross Primary School, Whitecross

Anger

Anger is red
It smells like smoke
Anger tastes like burning fire
It sounds like a kettle boiling
Anger feels like a hot iron.

Lorne Muldoon (11)
Whitecross Primary School, Whitecross

Sadness

Sadness is grey
Sadness smells like rotten bananas
Sadness tastes like quiche
Sadness sounds like a riot
Sadness lies in the heart of flames.

Jordan Braes (10)
Whitecross Primary School, Whitecross

Happiness

Happiness is yellow like the sun
It smells like spring flowers
Happiness tastes like ice cream with syrup
It sounds like birds chirping in a tree
It feels light and soft.

Jason Miller (11)
Whitecross Primary School, Whitecross

Happiness

Is pink
It smells like strawberries
Happiness tastes like fruit
It sounds like laughing
Happiness lies in sunshine.

Stacey Hunter (11)
Whitecross Primary School, Whitecross

Happiness

Happiness is bright yellow
It smells like fresh air
Happiness tastes like fresh strawberries
It sounds like birds tweeting all day
Happiness feels like baby oil running across your face.

Lisa McNeill (10)
Whitecross Primary School, Whitecross

War

War is black
It smells like dry blood
War tastes like death
It sounds like cannons firing
War lies in the field.

Christopher Smith (11)
Whitecross Primary School, Whitecross

Happiness

Happiness is pink
It smells like roses
Happiness tastes like strawberries
It sounds like laughing
Happiness lies in your arms.

Jodie Dalglish (11)
Whitecross Primary School, Whitecross

Young Writers

2004 POETRY COMPETITION

ONCE UPON A RHYME

Children often come to poetry with somewhat negative preconceptions. Encouraging them to write poems, and read those written by their peers, brings poetry to life and demonstrates its value as a powerful means of expression. Having their work published in a book alongside that of their peers in the region provides young people with a sense of achievement and gives them greater confidence in their creative writing ability.

Young Writers have been running their annual regional poetry competition in conjunction with schools for twelve years, to encourage the reading and writing of poetry by young people. The books produced represent a generation of voices having their say on a wide range of themes from home and school, to the environment and politics.

£14.99 UK
ISBN 1-84460-593-0

9 781844 605934

Edited by Annabel Cook

Visit our website: www.youngwriters.co.uk